Arbortext 101: Best Practices for Configuring Authoring, Styling, and Publishing with Arbortext

An Arbortext Monster Garage Book

Elizabeth Fraley

SECOND EDITION

Edited by: Lori Meyer and Kelly Schrank

Published by: Single-Sourcing Solutions

PO Box 62122, Sunnyvale, CA 94089.

www.single-sourcing.com

info@single-sourcing.com

www.twitter.com/SingleSourcing

ISBN: 978-0-9976505-1-8

First edition: 2016

This book was written in DITA using Arbortext Editor and published for print, PDF, ePub, and MOBI using Arbortext Styler.

Arbortext Monster Garage Books

Arbortext for Authoring: An Author's Guide to Getting Started with Arbortext Editor

Arbortext 101: Best Practices for Configuring, Authoring, Styling, and Publishing with Arbortext

Arbortext 102: Best Practices for Creating Arbortext Styler Stylesheets

TC Dojo Books

Adding Custom Actions to OxygenXML Frameworks

To anyone who was ever told by a consultant that it would be too difficult for you to do it yourself.

Contents

Chapter 1. About this book

Topics Covered in this Chapter

- ♦ Applicable software versions
- ♦ Acknowledgements
- ♦ About the author

The toughest thing about learning any new software package is making the shift from what you already know to how this new software replaces processes and changes your world. It's shifting from how you think it should fit into your world to how your world will adapt to it so you can use it most effectively.

All software vendors have expectations of how their applications fit into your world. This expectation appears most obviously in the help files and user documentation. The vocabulary in the help files can be daunting to new users of a technology, especially a complex one.

Say that we want to set up the security for a new environmental system we just purchased. When we look up "security" in the documentation index, we are directed to topics like "Access Control Lists" and permissions settings. We understand that those things are indeed "security" concerns, but we've been tasked with setting up the video cameras for building security. We are thinking "security"—but the help files come from a perspective that assumes we are approaching the task as an insider where the term "security" is a far lower technical task.

This disorientation is a situation we've all found ourselves in, especially when we are approaching a new product or a new technology that we are experts in. For most people, learning about something new is as much about learning how to think about the components of the new system in the way the vendor does so that their explanations make sense. Each vendor has a vocabulary all their own, like a micro-language. The people who write the documentation for that product or technology are experts in it—but their vocabulary may or may not be familiar to us.

It's one of the first battles we fight as a user of a new product or technology. We must struggle with someone else's vocabulary and orient ourselves to view the world as the vendor and product expect us to. In fact, the longer the company has been around, the harder it can be to find documents that streamline the adaptation process for new users. Content only grows and, with it, the assumption that users have some familiarity.

From the company's perspective, it makes sense: Didn't they write that brand-new user orientation stuff way back when the software was new? Isn't it still in there somewhere? It hasn't changed. So, it doesn't need updating. Right?

The Arbortext Product Suite is no exception. The company launched in 1991[1] and if you look at the 6.1 F000 release, you will find that Arbortext shipped with 18 manuals totaling nearly 5000 pages covering all aspects of authoring, styling and publishing using the Arbortext products. If we include all the documentation about managing content using Windchill, the count easily doubles.

The complete Arbortext documentation set covers a lot more than the basics. One of Arbortext's strengths is that it is a highly

1. wayback.arbortextuser.org

extensible, customizable, application suite. It has a full application programming interface (API) so customers who need the flexibility can develop applications on top of it. Nearly every part of all the applications that make up the Arbortext suite can be reached, adjusted, and tweaked by way of the API. Version 7.0 even has a full-blown integrated development environment (IDE) to help you with stylesheet source edits and advanced programming.

That's a lot of reading! And if you're new to the system, it can be hard to determine how much you need to know before you feel that you've set everything up correctly and in the best possible way.

Don't let that scare you!

Most Arbortext customers never create custom applications or dig into the API. You're more likely to make source edits in the stylesheets, but even that isn't common. These features provide flexibility for those who need them (and when they need them, they really need them).

Typically, Arbortext works right out of the box to handle 90% of technical documentation needs—user manuals, API documents, maintenance manuals, product guides, release notes, quick reference guides, software manuals, training manuals, study guides, legislation publications, and many more. For documentation needs that fall into the exotic 10%, the Arbortext suite provides additional applications that can handle that content.

If you're a new Arbortext user and feel that most of your technical publication needs are similar to 80-90% of technical publications out there, this book is for you. Even if you have more complicated needs, this book will give you a deep understanding of the Arbortext suite, with real-world examples of how each application is used, to help you get started in the right direction.

It doesn't matter what industry or what country you're in: Customers in every industry around the world use Arbortext. We're going to show you how to get started quickly and how to shift your understanding so that you can make the most of your investment in your world.

This book came out of our experience with customers who started with us, and those who came to us later after working with other channel partners. At Single-Sourcing Solutions, we are all former Arbortext users and our experience with Arbortext, XML publishing, and single-source authoring goes back nearly two decades. We became Arbortext Channel Partners in 2007 and, until experience was no longer considered the determining factor, we were an Authorized Training Partner for the Arbortext Product Suite. We still train, but we train the way the users need to use the product, not the "PTC" way.

This book is designed to help you orient yourself so that you can understand the concepts the Arbortext documentation writers are trying to convey. We will give you the vocabulary you need to search the help files quickly and efficiently. We'll also give you pointers about how to get started when you're ready to do more.

Applicable software versions

This book is current as of Arbortext 7.0 M050 (released 8 December 2016) and assumes PTC Server 11.0 F000 or higher (released 17 December 2015).

> **Expert tip!**
>
> With the M050 release PTC repositioned Arbortext under the Servigistics product line. For several releases starting with 7.0 M50 version, Arbortext was officially known as "Servigistics Arbortext." PTC dropped the "Servigistics" again later on when they shuffled their product portfolio.

This book was written in Arbortext Editor and published with Arbortext Styler. Our examples assume a local installation of Arbortext Editor and Styler. Where appropriate, we will provide information for alternate installations, but what we describe here is the foundation for any advanced deployment.

And anyone can do it.

Acknowledgements

Knowledge is sometimes tribal and Arbortext knowledge is no different. At Single-Sourcing Solutions, we have all benefitted from the knowledge of those around us. We started as customers. We have always done everything we can to share our knowledge with the world around us.

I want to thank Janice Summers, who has been essential to me over the years. Single-Sourcing Solutions has succeeded greatly due to her partnership with me (as well as my own growth). She’s a great coach and friend. Without her, I could not have done half as much as I have over the years.

Thanks to Lori Meyer, my editor and friend. She’s always encouraging and helped me find my voice. And to Kelly Schrank, without whom, there would be no index, something I noticed was missing when I went to use it.

Thanks to all of our customers for encouraging me to write this book and make it available for anyone who wants to learn how to use Arbortext to their best benefit.

I couldn’t have done it without any of you.

About the author

Elizabeth Fraley is a serial entrepreneur. She's founded two companies, sits on the boards of three non-profits, and is constantly coming up with new ways to share knowledge in the technical communications and content industries.

She works as a Single-Source/XML Architect/Programmer and Mentor. She has worked in industries ranging from high-tech to government, at companies of all different sizes (from startups to huge enterprises). She advocates approaches that directly improve organizational efficiency, productivity, and interoperability. She takes an apprentice to journeyman approach with her customers, holding their hands and enabling them to stand on their own two feet. She knows that her customers want to do it themselves and that they just don't want to do it alone.

A long time Arbortext customer, she constantly looks for ways to make tribal knowledge...not so tribal. She presents regularly at international, national, and regional conferences related to content, information architecture, and technical communication. Her appearances and publications are consistently well received by her peers. She created two community-driven webinar series (the Arbortext Monster Garage and the TC Dojo), three YouTube Channels, and an Arbortext On Demand Vimeo channel. She has an Arbortext Community Voices podcast and runs the Arbortext Meetup Group, LinkedIn Group, and Facebook group. She writes blog posts and publishes papers that enable the people in her communities. She developed the first techcomm mastermind series and, as president of Single-Sourcing Solutions, saved an internationally known Arbortext code archive from deletion. She's the founder of TC Camp, is the only unconference focused on the technical writing community and the people who support them.

Chapter 2. The Arbortext Product Suite

Topics Covered in this Chapter

- ♦ Purchasing Arbortext software
- ♦ Licensing Arbortext software
- ♦ Installing Arbortext

The Arbortext Product Suite offers solutions at every stage of information development: from defining, authoring, and illustrating to managing and delivering content. Arbortext is an end-to-end product information delivery system that automates the authoring and publishing processes for the delivery of high-quality, tailored product information in the form of operator manuals, service documentation, and eLearning courseware.

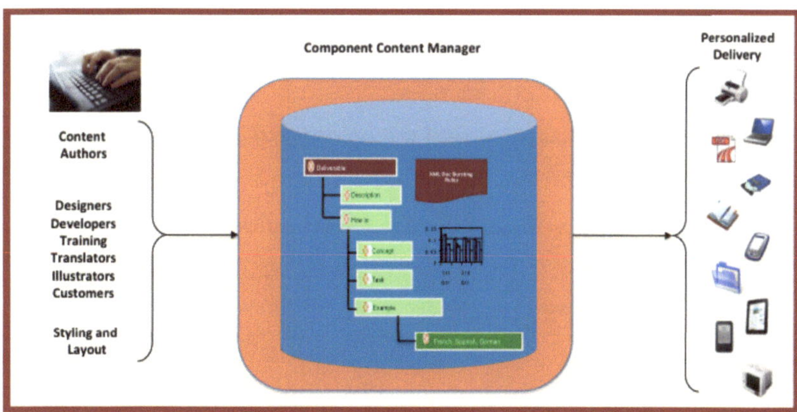

Deployed as a complete integrated product information delivery system, the components of the Arbortext Product Suite are built and tested together, to ensure out-of-the-box deployment with low risk, easy upgrades, and a low total cost of ownership.

Most customers purchase a subset of the Arbortext Product Suite. Everyone needs to create content (authoring), design the look and feel of finished output (styling), create final publications (publishing), and manage all of those content units (content management).

A typical Arbortext deployment includes the following products in the Arbortext Product Suite:

Arbortext Editor (authoring)	A familiar word processing interface that makes it easy for authors to create and edit structured XML and SGML content for reuse and automated publishing.
Arbortext Styler (styling)	Enables publication designers to create multi-channel XML-based stylesheets for automated publishing in a simplified user interface.
Arbortext Publishing Engine (publishing)	Automatically extracts XML and SGML content from file systems or content management systems, assembles that content for different audiences, and publishes the assembled content automatically to print, Web, PDF, Microsoft Word, HTML Help, and other media formats.

Arbortext Content Manager (content management)	One brand name for the PTC Server. It is an integral component of the PTC Dynamic Publishing System that provides a single source of information, maintains control at every component level, preserves component relationships, and provides configuration management capabilities to enable organizations to optimize their publishing process.
Arbortext eLearning Library (training)	Recorded versions of official Arbortext courses, broken down into one-hour segments that you can watch as often as you like. This video library includes training for all Arbortext products.

Expert tip!

Before PTC had subscription licenses, we recommended that new customers purchase a license for at least one seat of the Arbortext eLearning Library because it includes training material dating back to Arbortext 5.3. Although the user interface has changed over time, much of the earlier content is valuable because it can be more in-depth than later content. As of January 2018, all licenses are subscription and come with a free eLearning license.

With the release of later versions, the eLearning library course content has been updated to reflect changes to the application's user interface. However, as time marches on and XML technologies become more widely used and understood, PTC has dropped some of the foundational material (such as "what is xml?") from the course material. Because the technology hasn't changed, it is not repeated in later-version courses. We often recommend watching some of the older eLearning courses simply for the explanatory content.

Purchasing Arbortext software

Arbortext Editor, Styler, and Publishing Engine are currently available for Windows only. Arbortext Content Manager is available on multiple platforms. For details, check the Software Compatibility Matrix for the version you're looking to deploy. This matrix is updated with every release and is available with the rest of the documentation set on ptc.com.

PTC does not sell directly to users over the Internet, but they do have a large channel partner network of value-added resellers. Partners have different specialties and are assigned to geographic regions. You can find a reseller partner on the PTC website.

Expert tip!

We highly recommend that you select a qualified Arbortext partner for your purchase as well as for your service partner. These are the partners whose primary focus is the Arbortext Product Suite. They live it every day and know the tools inside out. However, even if PTC assigns you to a different reseller partner for purchasing purposes, you can still use one of these elite partners for services and consultation. You can get good advice from a services partner who has extensive experience with the Arbortext Product Suite.

To find a list of Arbortext qualified partners, look at the "Everything Arbortext in One Place" article on the Arbortext Users blog: everything.arbortextuser.org

Licensing Arbortext software

Anyone who will be authoring, editing, or working with source content requires a licensed copy of Arbortext Editor installed on their Windows computer.

Arbortext Styler is a concurrent license and can be shared among those who will be working on the stylesheets. The license floats: Only one person can use it at a time. Because stylesheets determine output, the ability to change them should be controlled in your environment and limited to only those people who will be working with the stylesheets.

Arbortext Publishing Engine is installed on a server. Arbortext Editor can be configured so that anyone who has a copy of Editor can publish content using Arbortext Publishing Engine.

Arbortext Content Manager is the component content management system and source repository. If you are using Arbortext Content Manager as your content repository, each user needs an individual seat license. Arbortext Content Manager can also be configured so that content can be published with Arbortext Publishing Engine directly from inside Arbortext Content Manager web client.

> **Expert tip!**
>
> We recommend choosing Arbortext Content Manager as your content repository because Arbortext Editor has a direct bridge into Arbortext Content Manager, making it easy to save, access, and reuse content. You don't need additional software or consulting services to connect your editing and publishing tools to your content management system!

Getting trial licenses

Trial licenses are available from the ptc.com website. Keep the following in mind: Licenses are valid for 14 days *from the date of download, not the date of installation*. It can take up to 2 *business* days to get your trial license from PTC, so be sure to take that into account before you download your trial on a

Friday afternoon. Only one trial license is available per MAC address, so you need to remember that, too.

If you require a longer trial, ask a channel partner. They may be able to help. Be aware that channel partners are required to have a valid business case to get an extended trial license issued by PTC. Channel sales teams must provide expected sales close dates and overall deal numbers for PTC to authorize an extended trial license.

Installing Arbortext

Arbortext Editor, Arbortext Styler, and Arbortext Publishing Engine are installed like any other Windows program. They are installed in the Program Files directory of your Windows computer.

Installation takes about 30 minutes, including licensing. Once the applications are installed, you can use Arbortext right out of the box.

We offer several configuration tasks as best practices to improve your experience (and simplify tasks for your IT team). Of these, the easiest one to get wrong is setting up your custom directory. The remaining configuration tasks are simple and straightforward. In the rest of this book, we will walk you through everything step by step. When we're done, you'll have Arbortext installed and configured to work in the best way possible...and you'll know everything the experts know about getting the foundation set up right.

The following four steps outline the best practices for setting up your Arbortext applications.

Expert tip!

In 2018, Oracle announced changes to their Java support policies which affect the Arbortext product line.

From the announcement PTC made in October 2018: *"Oracle has announced changes to their Java support policies effective January 2019 that affect many PTC products that use Java. After January 1, 2019, PTC will no longer be authorized to distribute non-publicly available versions of Java JRE (Java Runtime Environment) or the JDK (Java Development Kit) with product installations or in maintenance updates. As a result, post-January 2019, PTC will no longer distribute Java for any new product releases or any maintenance update, except for free trial and freemium products. For products released prior to January 2019, PTC may continue to distribute a publicly-available version of Java with the product release only. In all cases, customers will need to secure their own support contracts with Oracle starting in January 2019 to receive updates to Java for their PTC products and to install new versions of products"*

Chapter 3. Step 1: Set up your Arbortext custom directory

Topics Covered in this Chapter

♦ What's in the custom directory?
♦ How to identify a custom directory to Arbortext
♦ Let's Do It

Arbortext Editor, Arbortext Styler, and Arbortext Publishing Engine all use a simple and straightforward mechanism to process and execute any custom configurations, scripts, or application files that are specific to your company, publications, and requirements. This mechanism is called the Arbortext custom directory.

In the same way that XML authoring separates form from content, the Arbortext custom directory allows you to separate your custom configurations from the application source code. The custom directory gives you the flexibility to configure your Arbortext environment to meet your individual needs without customizing the Arbortext application in the traditional sense.

In Arbortext, the custom directory is a framework with several subdirectories where you can place custom script or application files and custom dictionaries, document types (including DITA specializations), fonts, graphics, entities, and other customizations. Each directory serves a particular purpose in the application initialization sequence, the document processing sequence, or the general user environment.

By creating your custom directory, you are telling Arbortext that the files in your custom directory should override any default behavior, style, or behavior in the out-of-the-box version. Arbortext will always look at your custom directory first. Only if it can't find what it needs will it fall back to the files contained in the application install tree.

Your custom directory should be placed *outside* the application install tree (Windows Program Files). With an external custom directory, you can do the following:

- isolate customizations so you can update without having to reinstall and reconfigure your systems
- use a layered approach to control corporate assets and branding, while still allowing individual users to customize their personal environment
- make everything available to individual users without constant IT maintenance tasks

By creating an independent custom directory structure, you can customize the application for your internal users without affecting the base Arbortext source code. You will be able to upgrade your software to take advantage of bug fixes without affecting your own implementation.

When a new feature comes along—for example, when the next version of DITA is ready—you will be able to upgrade Arbortext and get the new DITA features automatically without having to re-implement, reinstall, or reconfigure your entire environment. By locating your custom directory outside the install tree, you can upgrade Arbortext without risking clobbering or accidentally deleting your custom configurations, fonts, graphics, entities, or document types and specializations.

If you support multiple users and want their computers to be updated automatically, or if you want to add menus to applications running on their computers, the custom directory provides an externally accessed framework to do exactly that.

Setting up a custom directory structure will give you the undying appreciation of your IT support staff. They will be free to run upgrades on their timeline with little impact to you and everyone who uses the applications. In addition, the custom directory structure can go anywhere—on your computer, on a shared drive, or on a server. Putting it on a server has several benefits that IT folks understand, such as having a single location to manage rather than updating everyone's individual workstation. They will thank you for that.

To see a sample custom directory structure, look at the install tree in Windows Program Files, where you will see a custom directory that is created when you install Arbortext. This directory is for demonstration purposes only. It provides an example that you can use as a model to create your own custom directory structure in a safe location. If you use the custom directory structure inside the install tree, you risk accidentally losing all the work you did to make the Arbortext environment function the way you want it to.

You must be sure that you use the correct structure for your subdirectories in your custom directory. The subdirectory structure must be the same as that of the sample custom directory structure in the install tree. Having an incorrect structure won't cause problems operationally. Arbortext will simply ignore any directories that do not match those included in the sample.

You can have more than one custom directory as long as you specify the locations to the Arbortext application. Arbortext uses a Windows system environment variable named APTCUSTOM to store the locations of custom directories that should be sourced or executed.

The custom directory can be a physical directory or a compressed zip file of the physical custom directory structure. Both the directory and the zip file can be named anything you like. Just remember that the substructure *must be the same* as the default custom directory structure.

Expert tip!

A zip file deployment benefits maintenance and support across teams of multiple users and can make managing the custom directory easier. When you deploy the custom directory as a zip file, Arbortext Editor will look for any changes in the zip file whenever a user opens Arbortext Editor on their computer. If it finds changes, it will refresh the local cached files and retrieve any new content.

If you understand how to construct this framework and set it up right, you free yourself from the headaches often associated with customizing complex software systems.

Expert tip!

If you have deployed your custom directory as a zip file for Publishing Engine, you must restart Publishing Engine for the change to take effect.

What's in the custom directory?

The custom directory provides a structured framework for you to isolate your proprietary configurations, scripts, and files (including fonts, graphics, entities, and document types) within Arbortext. By creating your own custom directory, you can easily extend Arbortext and its operation.

As of Arbortext 7.0, the sample custom directory provided in the install tree looks like this:

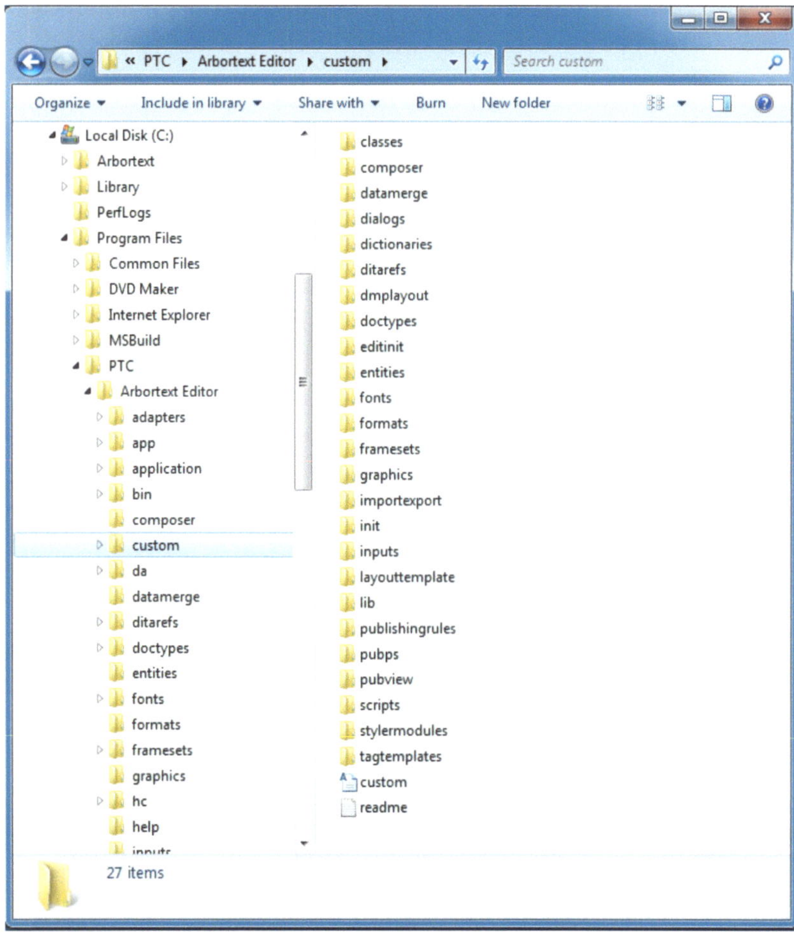

There are 27 possible subdirectories you can have in your custom directory. You can simply omit subdirectories you don't need. And if you discover later that you do need them, you can add them back as you go!

Many of these subdirectories come into play only in specific cases, but there are three that everyone uses. Whenever we set up a new customer, we always start with these three subdirectories:

- **doctypes**: Arbortext Editor/Publishing Engine searches this directory for "catalog" files and doctype definitions.
- **graphics**: Arbortext Editor/Publishing Engine searches this directory for any unpathed references to graphics.
- **stylermodules**: Arbortext Editor searches this directory for stylesheet modules to process.

If we know that we'll be producing customized web output, we'll add one more directory: the **framesets** directory. (We won't be covering customizing web output in this book because it's an advanced topic that could be a book all of its own.)

We are mentioning this now because this is one directory that makes a frequent appearance in custom directories. And now, you know where to go when you are ready to take the next step towards customizing your web output!

- **framesets**: Arbortext Editor searches this directory for any frameset directories (specified in a .dcf file) for use with the **File→Compose→For Web...** feature.
- **ditarefs**: Arbortext Styler/Publishing Engine will look for referenced DITA content, like .ditaval files, in this directory.

Expert tip!

If you want more detail about the other directories, the sample custom directory includes a **readme.txt** file, which describes the directories and what they do. You can also consult the *Arbortext Customizer's Guide* from PTC for an in-depth discussion on each directory available in the custom directory structure.

Be careful when constructing your custom directory: the substructure must be exactly the same as the sample custom directory structure. If you don't construct your custom directory correctly, your files will not be available when you use the application. You can look at the sample custom directory provided in the install tree to verify that your custom directory structure is correct.

How to identify a custom directory to Arbortext

Arbortext uses a Windows system environment variable (APTCUSTOM) to store the locations of custom directories and the order in which they must be sourced or executed.

You can have one or more custom directories. For each custom directory, include paths to them by adding the paths to the environment variable. Specify each custom directory, in the desired order, as the value of APTCUSTOM. Be sure that the % H symbolic parameter is in path list to include default locations. The symbolic parameter %H identifies the default location and must be included. If you omit the default location, you will lose the installed doctypes. This omission can be especially problematic when dealing with DITA specializations.

Depending on where your custom directory is located and how you've constructed it, create a new system environment variable in one of three ways:

- The fully qualified path to a directory on your computer
- The fully qualified path to a directory on a server
- The fully qualified path to a zip file on your computer or on a server

Separate multiple paths with a semi-colon. Paths must be fully qualified. Relative paths and uniform resource locators (URLs) are not supported.

For your computer

- **Variable Name**: APTCUSTOM
- **Variable Value**: %H%;<path>

For a server

- **Variable Name**: APTCUSTOM
- **Variable Value**: %H%;\\servername\path\to\Arbortext \custom\

For a zip file on a server

- **Variable Name**: APTCUSTOM
- **Variable Value**: %H%;\\servername\path\to\Arbortext \<zipfile>.zip

Let's Do It

Now that we know what to do and where to go for more information, let's do it!

Create the directory substructure:

1. Create C:\Arbortext
    a. Create C:\Arbortext\custom
    b. Create C:\Arbortext\custom\doctypes
    c. Create C:\Arbortext\custom\graphics
    d. Create C:\Arbortext\custom\stylermodules
    e. (Optional) Create C:\Arbortext\custom\ditarefs
    f. (Optional) Create C:\Arbortext\custom\framesets

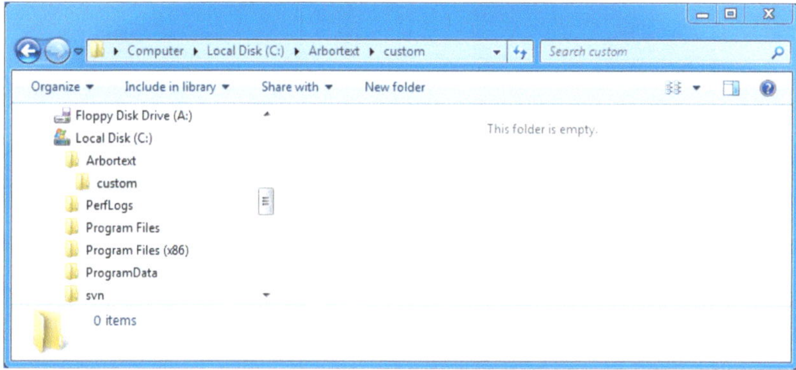

Create the APTCUSTOM environment variable:

- **Variable Name**: APTCUSTOM
- **Variable Value**: %H%;C:\Arbortext\custom\

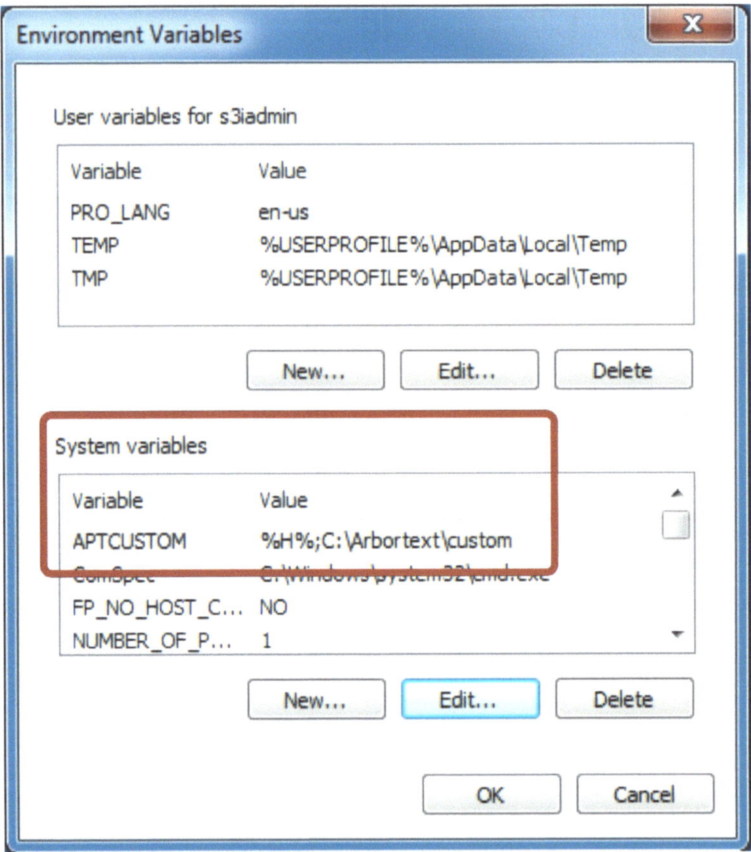

Launch Arbortext Editor and verify that Arbortext Editor is connecting to your custom directory. From the **Help** menu, choose **Session.** In the custom directory path you should see **C:\Arbortext\custom**. It will show only the paths to directories you've added in the APTCUSTOM variable value. It will not show path variables.

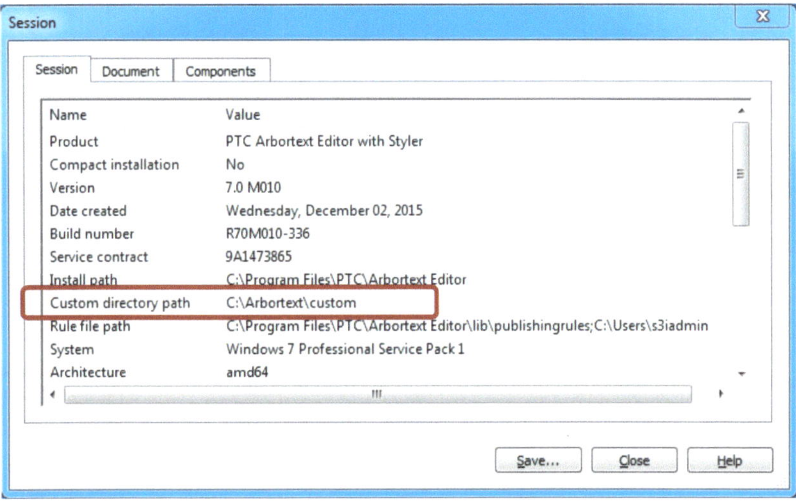

Now that our custom directory is ready, let’s fill up some of those directories!

Chapter 4. Step 2: Add files to your custom directory

Topics Covered in this Chapter

- ♦ The graphics directory
- ♦ The stylermodules directory
- ♦ The framesets directory
- ♦ The ditarefs directory
- ♦ The doctypes directory
- ♦ Let's Do It

Once your custom directory is set up and with the environment variable pointing to the right place, the next step is to add the right files in your custom directory and build the foundation for your needs.

Arbortext ships with files you can use for your foundation, including sample stylesheets, scripts, and code you can use to get started.

In the last example, we set up these three subdirectories:

- doctypes
- graphics
- stylermodules

Each subdirectory serves a specific purpose for Arbortext Editor, Arbortext Styler, and Arbortext Publishing Engine. Putting relevant files for your specific authoring and publishing needs into each one will give you a solid foundation for future work. We'll now look at each one and show you what goes where.

The graphics directory

This directory serves as the fallback location for graphics files used by Editor, Styler, and Publishing Engine. While you can store graphics here, it is not meant to be a replacement for a content repository.

The graphics directory is specifically for graphics needed for your doctype to function—the graphics declared in the document type definition (DTD or XSD). It is also the place to store graphics used in generated text in your stylesheet (either the in-Editor stylesheet or the stylesheet used for publishing through the Publishing Engine). Examples include your company logo and icons used for warnings, cautions, or notes.

The stylermodules directory

Arbortext supports modular stylesheets (stylesheets that can be created from modular components). A stylesheet module is a chunk that can be reused as needed in many stylesheets. In fact, any stylesheet can reference any other stylesheet as a module.

To keep things simple and to best facilitate the behavior that the Arbortext custom directory structure provides, put any new modules you create in the stylermodules directory. That way, you will have access to them for any stylesheet you create. This directory serves as the fallback location for Arbortext to find modules used in your stylesheet. Arbortext expects to find your Styler stylesheet modules in the stylermodules directory.

The stylermodules directory in your custom directory overrides the default stylermodules directory found in the install tree. If you installed Editor and Styler using the “Typical” configuration, you can find the default stylermodules directory here: *C:\Program Files\PTC\Arbortext Editor\stylermodules*

One of the great things about the way the Arbortext custom directory structure functions is that you can use the modules provided in the default stylermodules directory. This directory provides lots of sample Styler modules that you can use in your stylesheets. Because PTC maintains these files, you will get the updated modules when you update your Arbortext installation.

If you are using DITA, there are special benefits for using DITA stylesheets. With DITA, you want to incorporate the default stylermodules as the basis for any stylesheet you create. Why? Because as the DITA standard evolves and PTC adds support for all the new DITA elements, you will get formatting for all the new elements automatically for free!

PTC provides support for all DITA elements and attributes for editing and publishing. Although the default formatting is the formatting that PTC has created, it is included automatically. Some elements might be unformatted or might use fallback processing from their base elements, but every element will have some amount of coverage. This means your authors can use new DITA elements as soon as the specification advances and your Arbortext software is updated. In addition, you can publish that content long before your stylesheet catches up!

As long as you use the default DITA style module provided by Arbortext, you'll be protected and able to support your authoring and publishing requirements without additional startup work.

We're not going to put anything in the stylermodules directory right now because we haven't created any modules. Even though creating stylesheets and stylesheet modules is an advanced topic for another book, we still want to have this directory set up at the very beginning because we want to be ready! You'll find the ability to use modules in your stylesheet to be one of the most powerful tools in your stylesheet toolbox.

The framesets directory

The framesets directory serves as the primary location for customizing HTML and web output. If you chose to create this directory, put copies of the default frameset supporting code in this directory now.

Changing these files will change the way your output looks. By using the custom directory to store these files, you can guarantee that it will use your files instead of those provided out of the box.

We're not going to discuss editing and changing the frameset files now, because that's an advanced topic for another time. For now, the files you need to change the web output are ready and waiting for you!

The ditarefs directory

This directory serves as the fallback location for DITA content referenced by topic references, content references, DITAVAL files, and so on. This folder is not used for any content not based on the DITA doctype.

While you can store DITA content here, it is not meant to be a replacement for a content repository.

Expert tip!

In the install tree, this directory stores the files that are used to create sample files when the **Sample** option is selected in the **New File** dialog box. If you installed Editor and Styler using the "Typical" configuration, you can find these sample files in the default ditarefs directory here: *C:\Program Files\PTC\Arbortext Editor \ditarefs*

The ditaref directory and DITAVAL files

DITAVAL files are used for conditional processing. Arbortext already had the ability to do conditional processing when DITAVAL files were added to the DITA specification. Arbortext can use both DITAVAL files and .pcf files for conditional processing at publish time.

The .pcf file is the way to enable conditional processing in Arbortext Editor. If you use conditional processing and you want those conditions to be portable, you should have both .pcf and .ditaval files configured. The .pcf file will make it easy for your authors to add conditional processing; the .ditaval file will make your conditional processing portable.

For publishing, you can use either .ditaval files or .pcf files. If you want to use your .ditaval files, they must be stored in one of three places:

- The install tree
- The ditarefs subdirectory in your custom directory

- In the same folder as the DITA source content that should receive the conditional profiling

If you want to be able to reference DITAVAL files at publish time, you must put your .ditaval files in the ditarefs subdirectory of your custom directory.

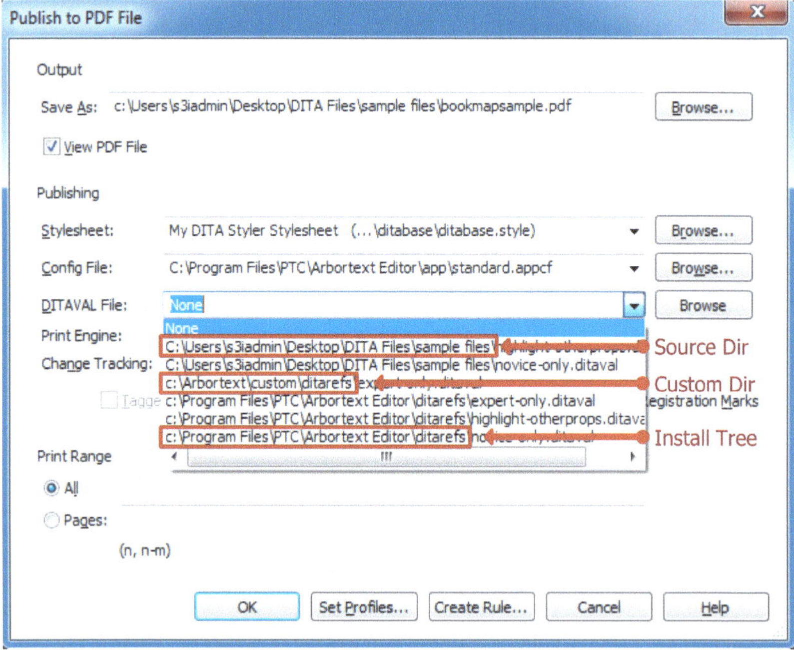

Expert tip!

We recommend that you replicate the conditional profiling of your .ditaval files in your .pcf file.

You get the ease of using the familiar Arbortext user interface to add the markup for conditional processing, while creating valid, portable DITA content that can be processed with the matching .ditaval files.

The doctypes directory

This directory is one of the most important directories in the custom directory but it is also the most complex to explain. That's why we saved it for last.

This directory is where you will put these items:

- DITA specializations or any customized DocBook doctypes
- S1000D, ATA, NLM, or other custom doctype definition files
- configuration files (editing, publishing, profiling) and the top-level stylesheets for each doctype

Three files are key to doctype configuration in Arbortext:

- Doctype Configuration File (.dcf)
- Profile Configuration File (.pcf)
- Default Stylesheet (.style)

What do these files do? Each file serves a specific function in the Arbortext environment. The Doctype Configuration File (. dcf) allows you to configure document "type-scoped" settings. The Profile Configuration File (.pcf) allows you to configure profiling settings for use in your created content. The stylesheet defines the look and feel for all of your output formats as well as the way content is displayed in the Editor.

Each of these files should have the same name as the doctype directory. For example, if you're using the Arbortext DocBook doctype (*axdocbook*), name the directory *axdocbook.* The .dcf file should be named *axdocbook.dcf*, the .pcf file should be named *axdocbook.pcf*, and the stylesheet should be named *axdocbook.style*. You'll see this in practice in a minute.

The doctype configuration file (.dcf)

Of these three files, the Doctype Configuration File (.dcf) file probably has the greatest impact to authors. In the .dcf file, you configure features in the Arbortext Editor user interface.

Want to turn off the **Touchup** menu for your authors? It's a simple change to the .dcf file that prevents the insertion of touch up code. Want to change the way element icons are displayed? Another simple .dcf tweak. Want to specify that certain elements have persistent file names when publishing web output? Again, just another .dcf tweak.

Take the **bold** button for example. We all know the familiar bold **B** button on the toolbar of our favorite document-editing tool. When you're authoring structured content, what should happen when this button is pressed? In DocBook, you should get *<emphasis role="bold"></emphasis>*. In DITA, you should get *<b></b>*. Maybe you want to outlaw the *<b></b>* markup in DITA and want to insert some other markup to discourage the use of it by your authors. You configure this in the .dcf file by telling it what tag/attribute combination to insert to make the selected text bold. By setting this in the .dcf file, you give users access to the familiar **B** button while still making sure that the right things happen automatically in the markup.

The .dcf file enables you to set configuration requirements for your DTD and preferences for your environment without having to do programming-heavy customization. It's portable and backward compatible as you upgrade your Arbortext software. It takes things that would otherwise be customizations and makes them configurations instead. This ability to use a configuration file is one of the biggest strengths of the Arbortext Product Suite.

Here are some settings you can change in the .dcf file:

- Application toolbar functionality
- Published print process
- Document-level formatting
- Default file extension
- Custom dictionaries
- Document editing restrictions
- Alternative directories for stylesheets, tag templates, frameset templates, etc.
- Document type Schematron file
- Equation support
- DITA ID assignment and other type-scoped settings specific to DITA document types
- Settings for specific element traits (character substitution, spell check ignored elements, hidden elements, empty element warnings.)
- Attribute display and properties that apply only to certain elements

Think of the .dcf file as a document type configuration file. Arbortext Editor provides many advanced features that make it easier to use and make it more comfortable for authors coming from other environments like Microsoft Word. Arbortext Editor has all the same features you typically find in Word, but to make Editor perform all of the same actions easily, it needs to know a few things about your DTD or Schema.

Because there are so many things you might want to change in the user interface and in the Arbortext environment, it's handy to have the .dcf file available so you can adjust it to your team's needs.

Most of the time you won't need to change the .dcf file. If you're using DITA or DocBook, you probably won't need to change the .dcf file unless you're specializing. It's still a good idea to have a copy of this file in your custom directory so that it's available should you need to make any changes.

The profile configuration file (.pcf)

The Profile Configuration Files (.pcf) specifies profile values that let you indicate the circumstances that dictate when certain parts of your document apply. By setting a profile, you can tell the publishing chain to include or exclude a section of content.

Profiles can specify that certain parts of your document be targeted to a specific audience or apply only when certain circumstances exist. Profiles can be applied to any element (or subset of elements) in a document type.

In the .pcf file, you can define the individual profiles that authors can apply to elements at editing time. Then, at publishing time, you can invoke a profile to produce profiled output. You can specify things like:

- elements to which the profile is restricted (or from which it is restricted)
- subclasses, groups, related profiles
- allowable values

What does that mean? Let's look at an example. Say you have two versions of a set of instructions: one is for customer service technicians and one is for everyone. In the version for customer service technicians, you include extra steps the technicians need to do their job. In the version you publish publicly, you omit those extra steps because your audience doesn't need those instructions except under specific conditions—and you want customers in that situation to call customer service for assistance. Instead, you create two profiles—*internal* and *everyone*—because internal people can see the same content everyone can see *plus* the internal-only content. The internal-only content should be omitted only when you publish for *everyone.* Here is what it looks like:

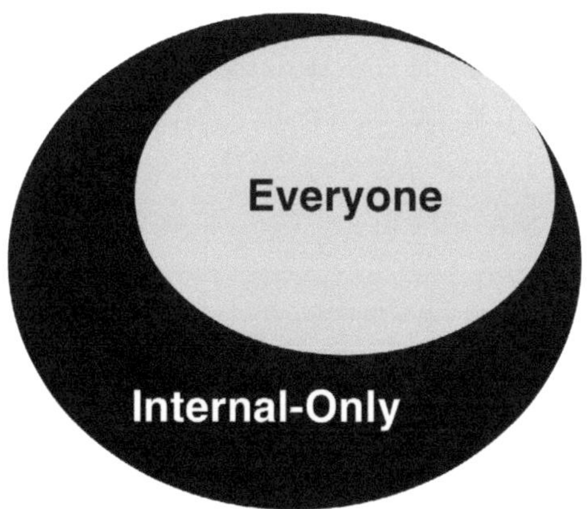

Internal people get extra information that is omitted when publishing the externally facing documentation. By creating a profile for *internal* and marking the internal-only information in your document with that profile, you mark that content for exclusion at publication time when you're publishing "for everyone."

It can be a powerful way to configure the level of detail in your content.

Arbortext invented the .pcf file as a way to provide for conditional processing during the publishing process. The .pcf file has existed in Arbortext since its earliest days and is valid for any doctype deployed in the Arbortext environment. The DITAVAL file in DITA is similar in function to the Arbortext .pcf file (which predates DITA).

The Arbortext .pcf file has special benefits for DITA because it existed before DITA had DITAVAL. They both function in a similar way. However, you can use the Arbortext profiling feature without having to specialize your DITA. Just use the .pcf file to set up your profile values: Change the .pcf file to reflect the profile values you want in your content and Arbortext will do the rest. Because the .pcf came first, Arbortext merged the correct behavior for the .pcf with DITA files as DITA matured, so everything does the right thing. Arbortext supports the use of the DITAVAL file, but it still supports .pcf files, too.

The default doctype stylesheet

In addition to the .dcf and .pcf files, every doctype has a default stylesheet. The Default Doctype Stylesheet has the same name as the doctype and it's the one that Arbortext looks to first when displaying content in the Editor or at publish time.

If a doctype does not have a default doctype stylesheet, Arbortext will attempt to find one in the install tree. For DITA, this means it defaults to the out-of-the-box DITA stylesheet that ships with Arbortext. For DocBook, it uses the out-of-the-box DocBook stylesheet. If you have a custom stylesheet, you will need to create a stylesheet so your authors get something more than tags to look at when they're authoring.

Because we don't want to contaminate the install tree, we can copy the out-of-the-box stylesheets into our custom directory. Then, we can change them to match our requirements. We can still roll back our changes to the default stylesheet because they will always be in the install tree. It's a good idea to grab the out-of-the-box stylesheets when we're setting things up so we don't have to worry about accidentally doing something that will hurt us later on.

If you make changes to these three files and then decide you want to get rid of all your changes, you can delete them then copy fresh versions from the install tree. By making copies of these files and putting them in your custom directory, you always have the originals as a back up. You can change the files in your custom directory at any time.

> **Expert tip!**
>
> For the full list of .dcf configuration options, search for "Document Type Configuration Files" in the Help Center.

Let's Do It

We're going to set up the standard DITA and DocBook doctypes in this example, while we fill out the basic set of files that can help us going forward.

Copy graphics to your custom directory

Now that we know what this directory is for, let's put a few files in here to get started.

Navigate to the graphics directory in your custom directory.

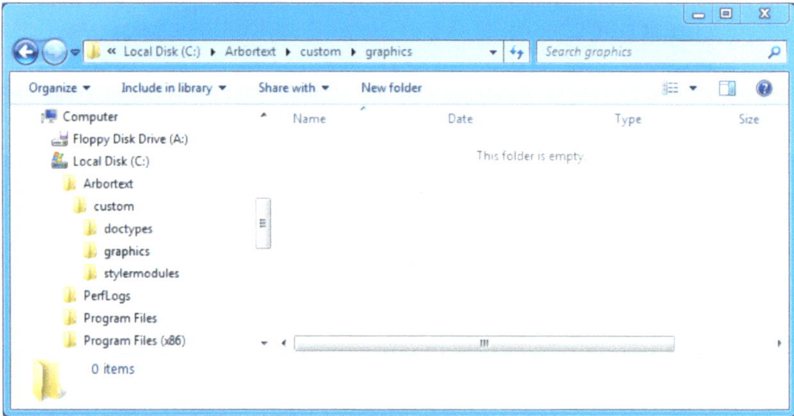

Copy your company logo graphic file into the directory.

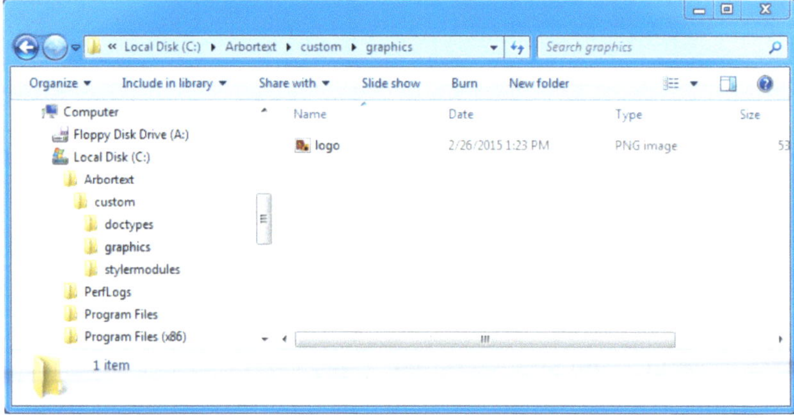

You can also copy the following files into this directory:

- Note, caution, and warning graphics files
- Full-page cover page graphic file

- Product logos
- Other corporate graphical content

Expert tip!

We strongly recommend that you put only corporate-level graphics in this directory. It's generally good practice to consider any graphics in this directory to be graphics whose main purpose is to support the stylesheet either in the Editor or in any of the published output formats.

Copy the default frameset to your custom directory

Let's get the necessary files in here so we can go about changing them!

Open a window and navigate to the framesets directory in your custom directory.

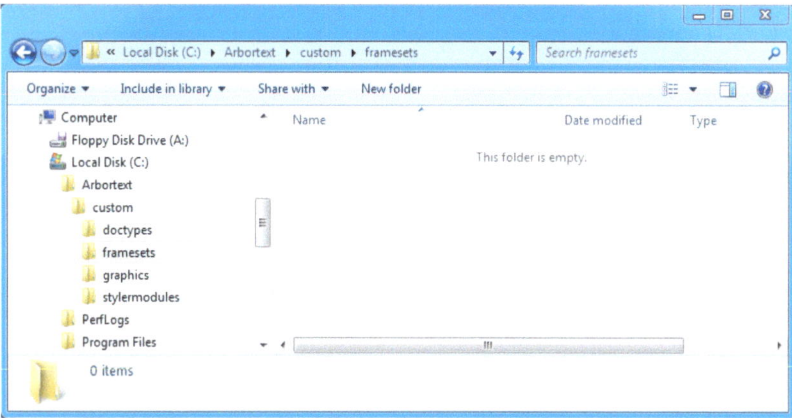

Open another window and navigate to the framesets directory in the install tree.

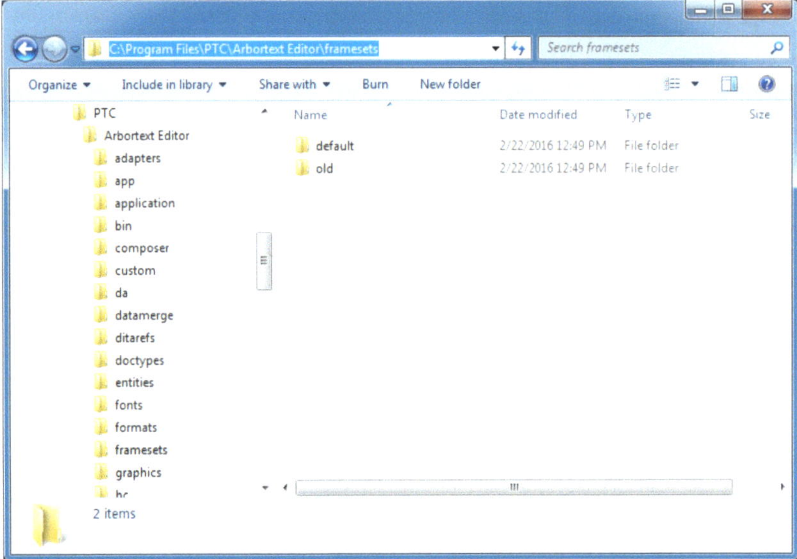

Copy the **default** directory from the install tree to your framesets directory.

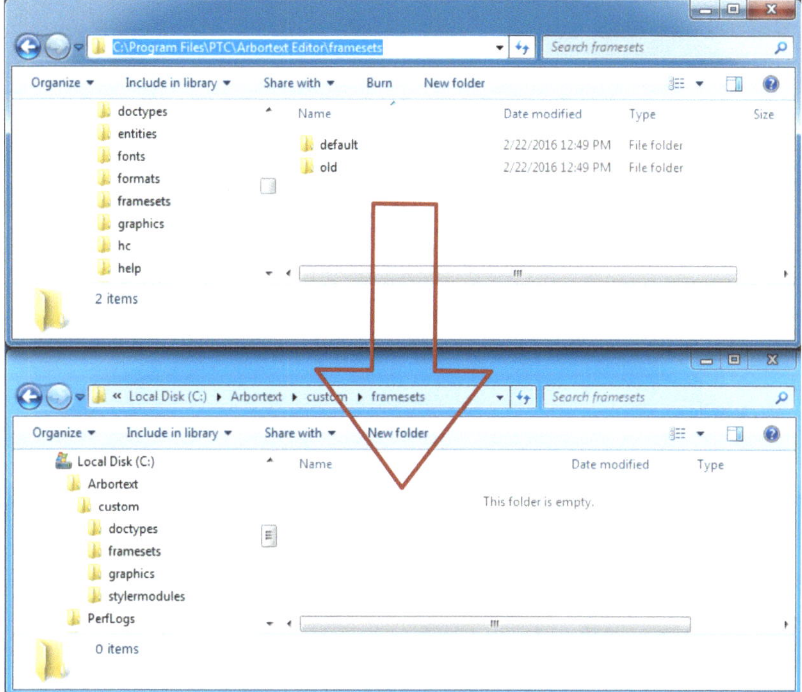

Edit the files in your custom directory to change look and feel of web output.

Copy default .dcf, .pcf, and .style files to your custom directory

Navigate to the doctype directory in your custom directory.

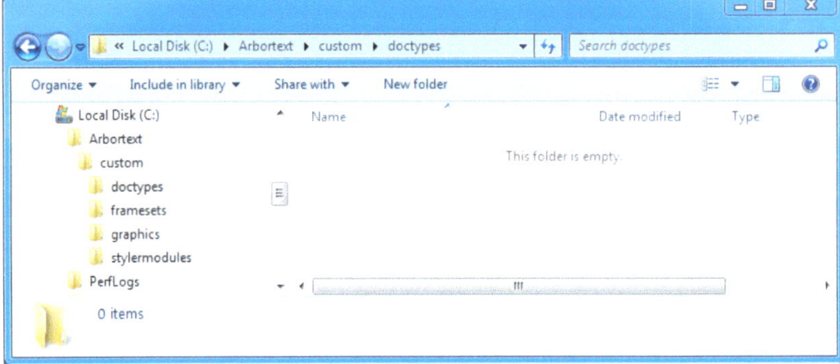

Create the directory substructure as follows:

- Create C:\Arbortext\custom\doctypes\axdocbook
- Create C:\Arbortext\custom\doctypes\ditabase

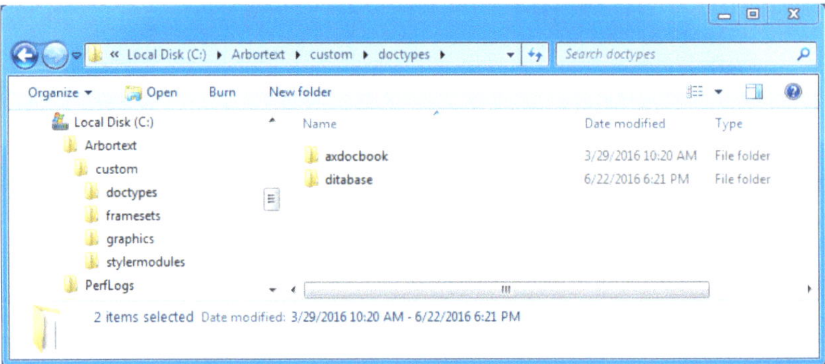

Open another window and navigate to the **axdocbook** doctype directory in the install tree.

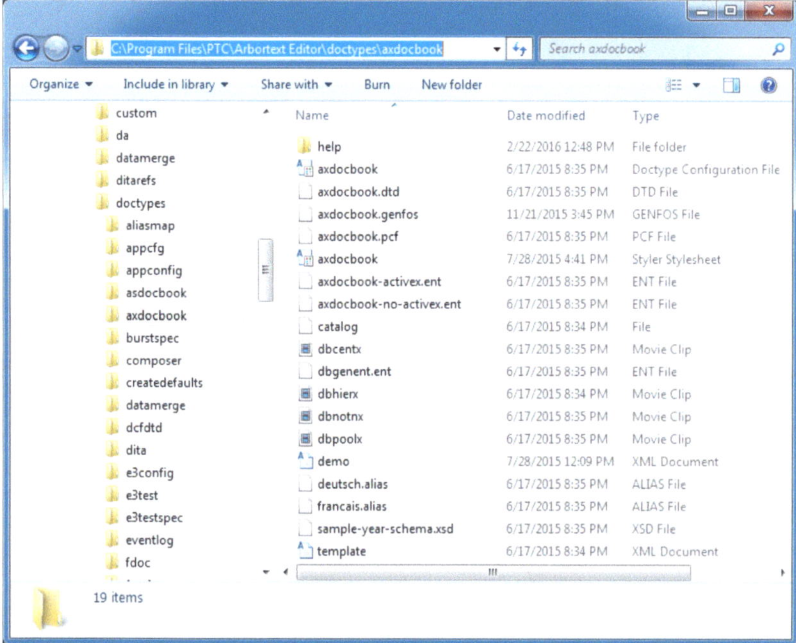

Copy the following files from the install tree into the **axdocbook** directory in your custom directory:

- axdocbook.dcf
- axdocbook.pcf
- axdocbook.style

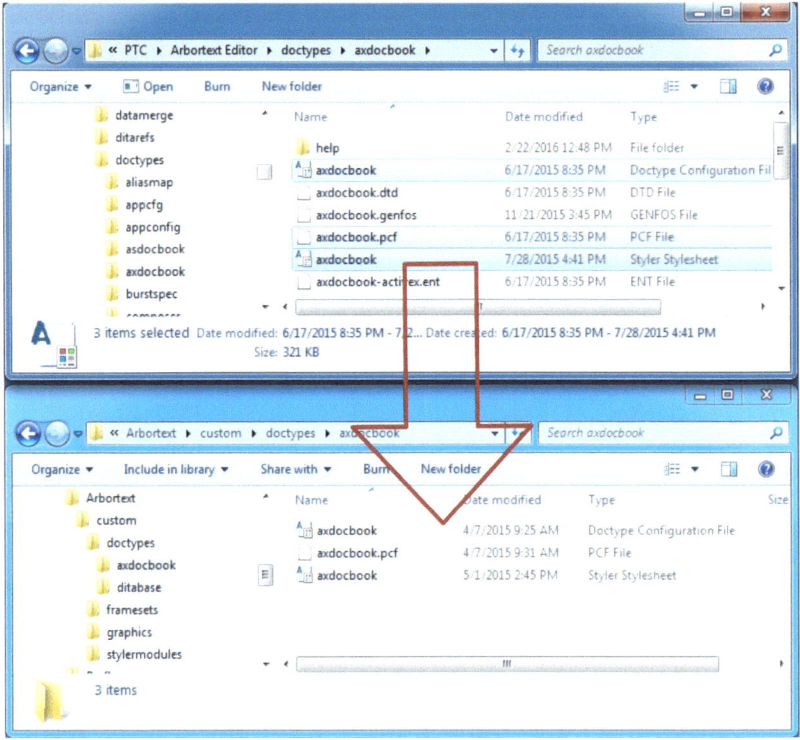

Navigate to the **ditabase** doctype directory in the install tree.

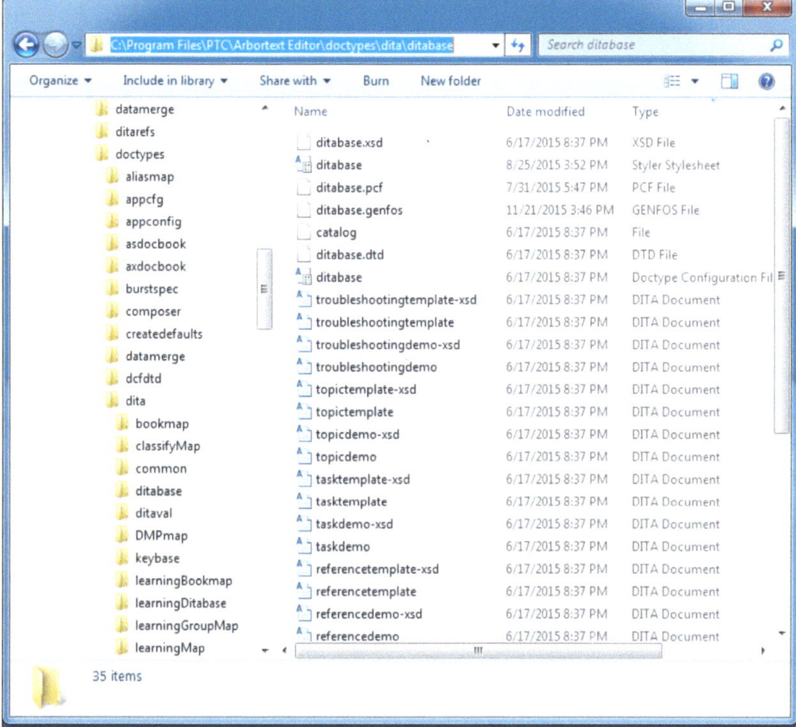

Copy the following files from the install tree into the **ditabase** directory in your custom directory:

- ditabase.dcf
- ditabase.pcf
- ditabase.style

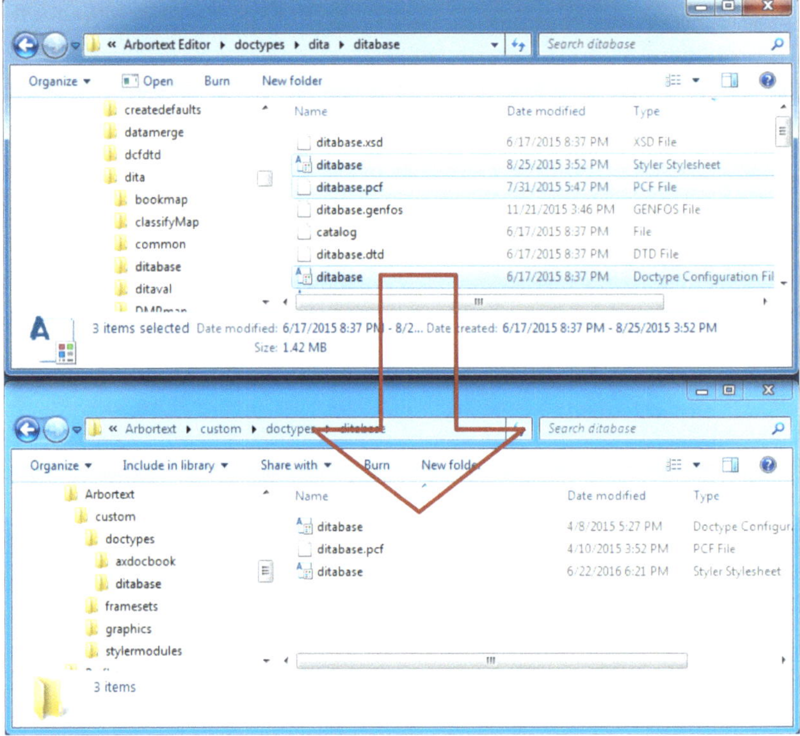

Change permissions on copied files

Right click on the doctypes directory. Choose **Properties**.

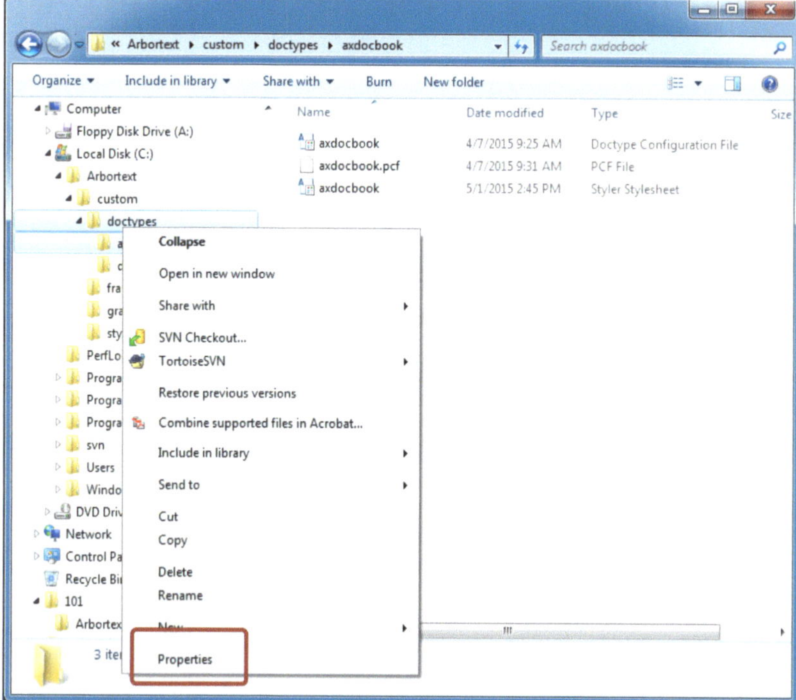

Be sure that the **Read-Only** property is clear and click **Apply**.

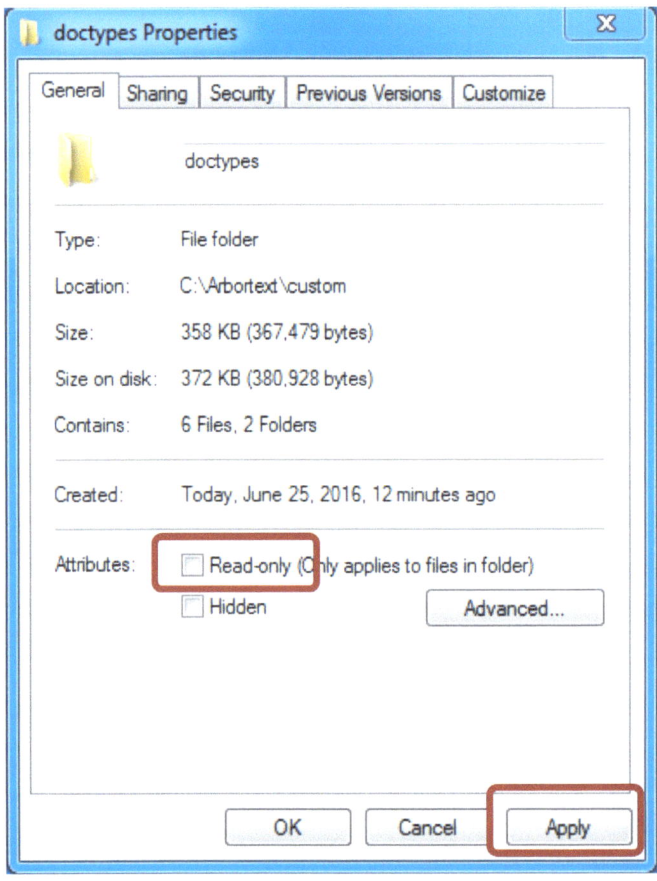

Click **OK** to confirm attribute changes and apply changes to this directory, all subdirectories, and files.

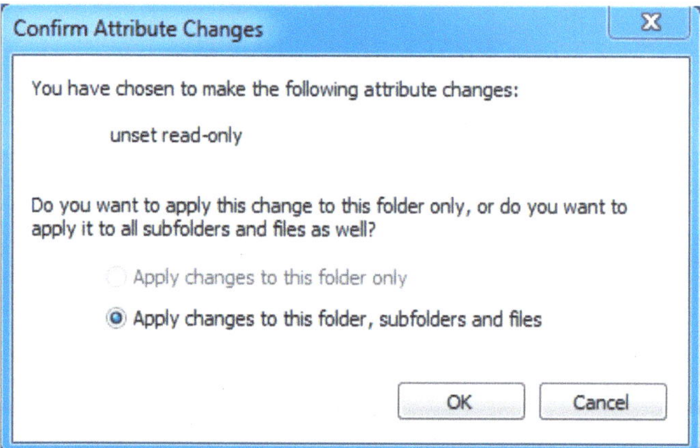

Confirm Attribute Changes
You have chosen to make the following attribute changes:
unset read-only
Do you want to apply this change to this folder only, or do you want to apply it to all subfolders and files as well?
Apply changes to this folder only
Apply changes to this folder, subfolders and files
OK
Cancel

Change the properties on the **framesets** directory so it is not marked **Read-Only**.

Chapter 5. Step 3: Set your user preferences

Topics Covered in this Chapter

♦ Turn on full menus
♦ Turn on the command line
♦ Change the color of generated text
♦ Remove processing instructions on file save
♦ Let's Do It

Several user preferences are useful to set early on so your authoring experience is easy when you're learning the tool. By changing your user preferences, you can customize the Arbortext Editor user interface and operation.

User preferences are set in the Preferences dialog box that is accessed from the **Tools** Menu. In this dialog box, you will find the preferences that are most frequently changed by users grouped into categories. You will also find an **Advanced** button that will give you access to every **set command** option that can affect the user interface and operation of Arbortext Editor.

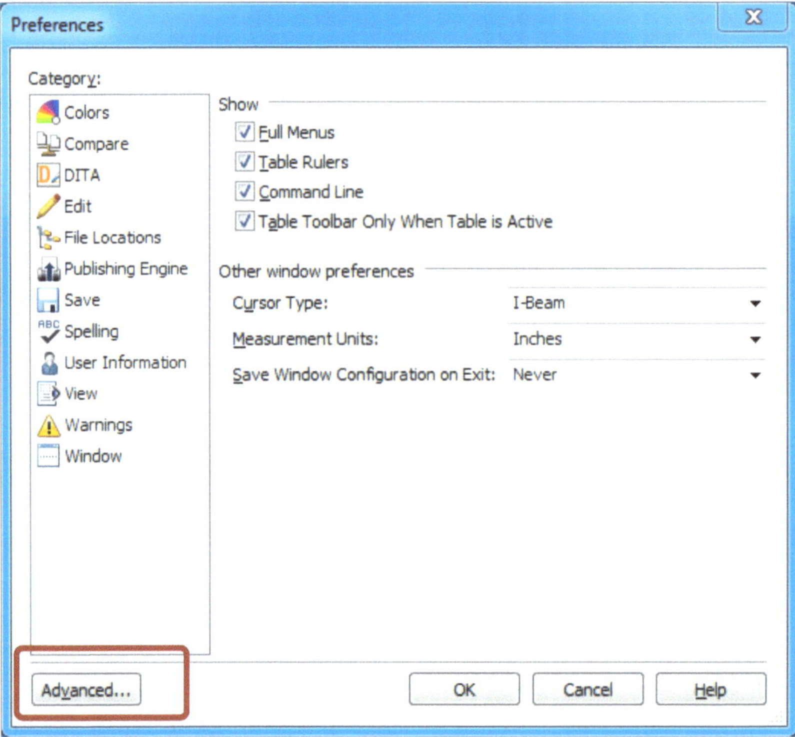

Changes to your user preferences are persistent. Changing any of these preference settings will affect the application every time you use it. You need to change these settings only once. We recommend the following:

1. Turn on Full Menus
2. Turn on the Command Line
3. Change the color of generated text
4. Remove processing instructions on file save

Many users feel comfortable exploring a new software application. Most of us know that if we don't know how to do something, we can try a few things. We can look around in the menu systems, consult the documentation, or search the web.

We know that if we look through the menu systems, we will very likely discover the key to doing whatever it is we're trying to do. We also know that we can consult the help files if our initial menu investigation fails.

Unfortunately, with Arbortext Editor's default installation, there's a good chance that when the first method fails (looking through the menus), we'll find a section in the help that tells us to go to a menu option that doesn't appear to exist. And a quick web search will tell us the same thing. We see that someone else has posted that it's in their menu...but, no matter how many times we look, we don't see it in our menu. This can be very frustrating.

The problem is that Arbortext Editor's default installation restricts the user interface to the basic authoring user interface with limited menus. No wonder you couldn't find it! It really wasn't there! Unfortunately, it also means that even if you go stepping through the menus, you're unlikely to find what you're looking for.

Luckily, there's a simple way to fix this problem. Change your preferences!

Turn on full menus

Changing your preferences to show Full Menus will give you access to more than the limited set that comes with the default installation.

With Full Menus on, you can settle in and get comfortable with the Arbortext Editor user interface knowing that when you go looking for a feature or function, you'll find it! Turning on Full

Menus means that the user interface will show you everything the menu system has to offer.

Turn on the command line

Turning on the command line gives you access to a command line that is a lot like the Unix or DOS command line. It gives you quick access to a lot of features, options, and help information.

The command line is particularly useful for locating information in the Help Center. Every page in the help has a unique topic number. Frequently, when you post a question to the user community, someone will answer by saying "See Help topic #NNNN" (where NNNN is the unique number for the help topic that answers your question).

To open that help topic, type *help NNNN* in the command line. The Help Center will open to that specific page. Want to try it out? Activate the command line and type **help 6923**. You'll get the help topic for .dcf files!

Change the color of generated text

Out of the box, both titles and generated text are blue in the Editor window. When you're learning, it's helpful to be able to differentiate text you can change from text you can't. Change the color of generated text to a different color like pink or brown. For new users, changing the color of generated text can be extremely helpful so they can differentiate the editable from the un-editable at a glance.

Changing the color for generated text in your preferences has no effect on the color of the generated text in published output.

Remove processing instructions on file save

This recommended preference change is something of a safety net. When you're first using Arbortext Editor, there are a lot of things to get used to. One of the toughest is resisting the urge to mix formatting and markup.

An important benefit of going to XML authoring and publishing is the ability to separate form from content. Published output is supposed to be governed by the rules specified in the stylesheet.

However, there are legitimate business cases where you need the fine control of things such as hard returns or non-breaking spaces. For those cases, Arbortext provides a Touchup menu.

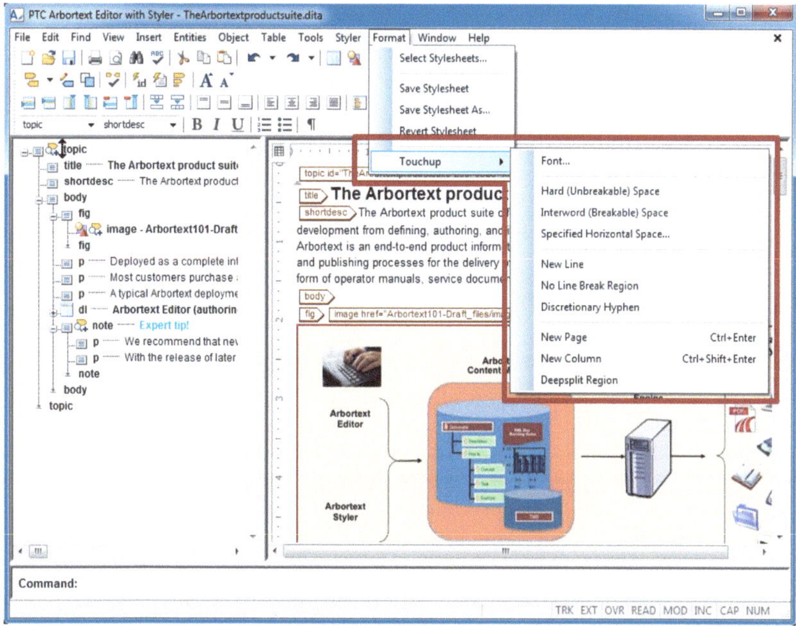

The problem is that users who come to Arbortext Editor from a desktop publishing background typically depend on using these kinds of tweaks in their regular running text. They are used to thinking and working in only one dimension: print output.

Arbortext source files are used for multiple output formats. They're an archive format not a delivery format. And even if your company is producing only PDF today, if you save touchup code in your XML source file, you'll never find all the instances to remove them tomorrow when suddenly your company wants HTML output. As a result, you'll get weird—looking HTML and will spend hours, if not days, trying to track it all down.

In addition, if you want to facilitate a new user's move to XML publishing and away from desktop publishing, it's a good idea to get rid of the temptation that allows them to do things that are detrimental down the road.

> **Expert tip!**
>
> By turning off the *writepi* setting, you make it impossible for them to save touchup code to their files, saving everyone a lot of heartache.

Let's Do It

We're going to change some basic preferences to make our lives a little easier.

How to turn on full menus and show the command line

Open Arbortext Editor. Go to the **Tools** menu and choose **Preferences**.

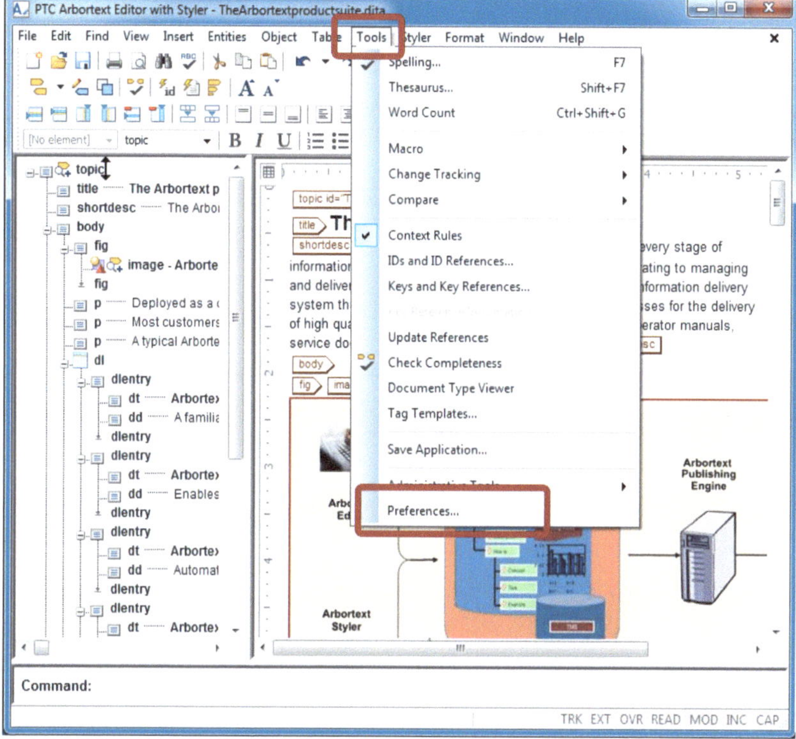

Select the checkboxes for **Full Menus** and **Command Line** and click the **OK** button

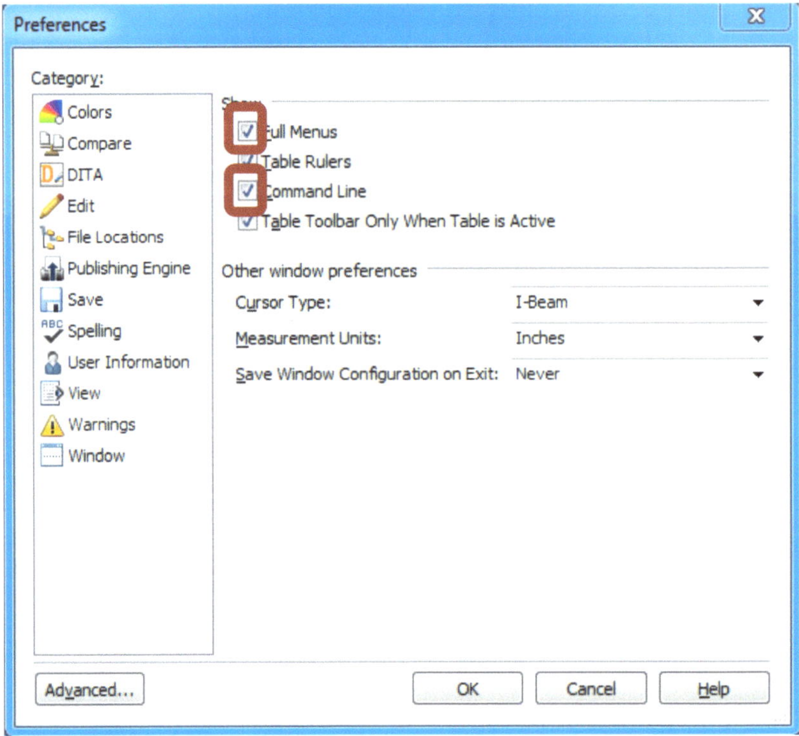

If you go back to Arbortext Editor, you'll see the command line at the bottom. If you look through the menus, you'll see more options, commands, and features at your fingertips.

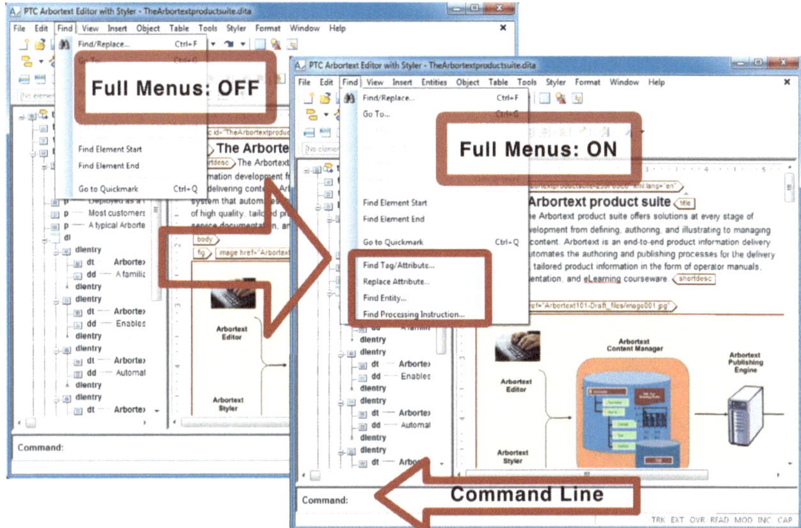

As you can see, you get four additional search methods when you turn on Full Menus.

How to change the color of generated text

Go to the **Tools Menu** and choose **Preferences**. In the Category pane, choose **Colors**. Click on the dropdown list next to **Generated Text**. Choose **Pink**.

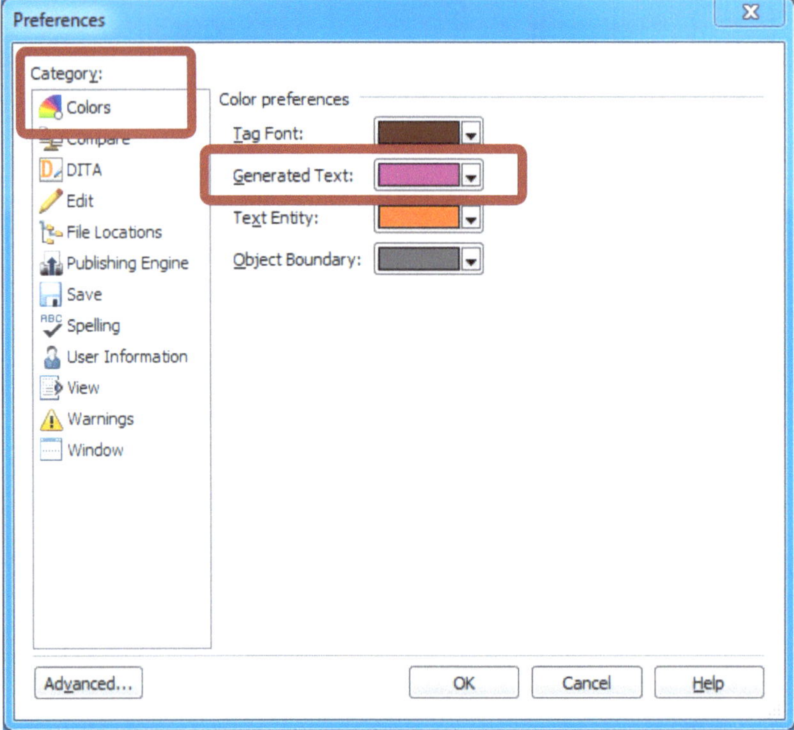

Click **OK** in the Preferences window to save your changes.

Changing the color of generated text to pink means that the generated text will appear pink in the Editor window. This change applies only to the generated text in the Arbortext Editor window. Changing this preference has no effect on any output generated in the publishing process. You can change color preferences to suit your individual needs and tastes.

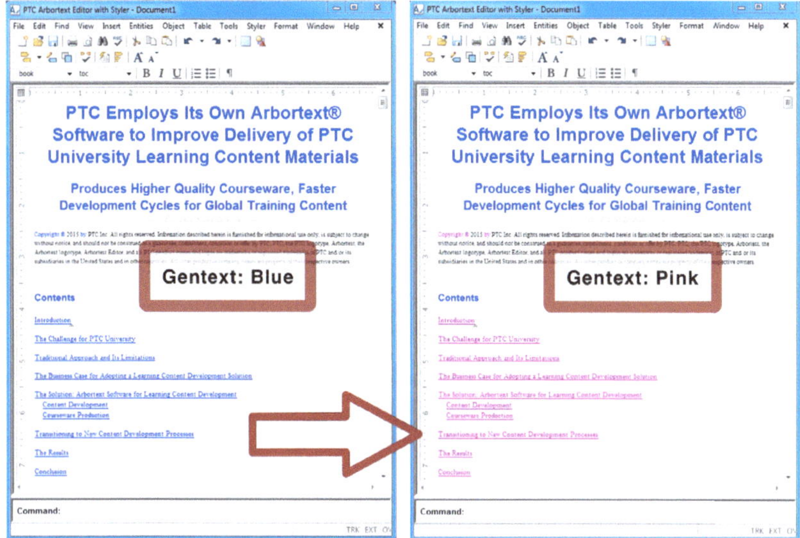

How to remove processing instructions on file save

Go to the **Tools Menu** and choose **Preferences**. Click **Advanced**.

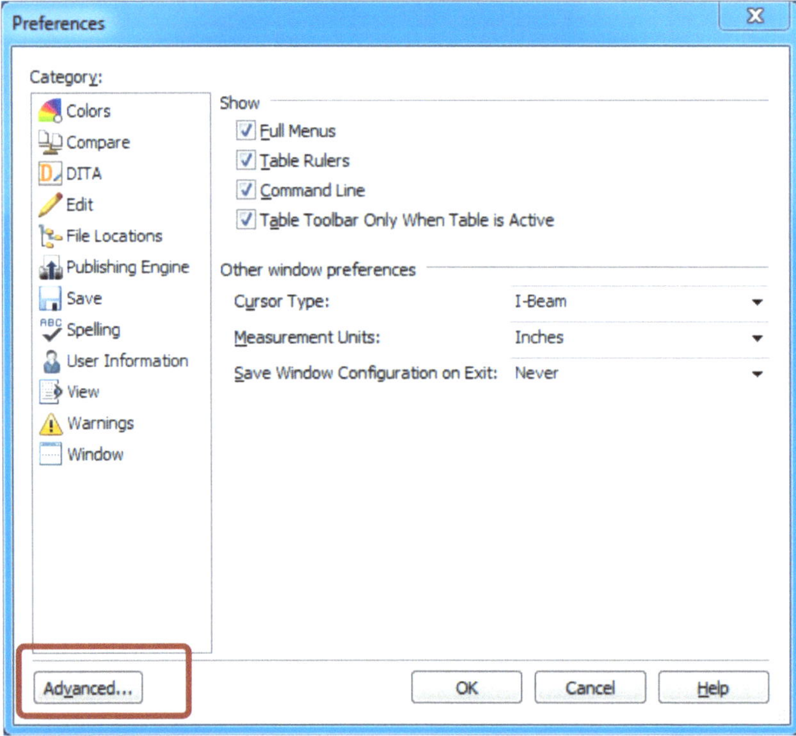

Scroll down until you see *writepi* in the Preference column. Select it and click **Edit**.

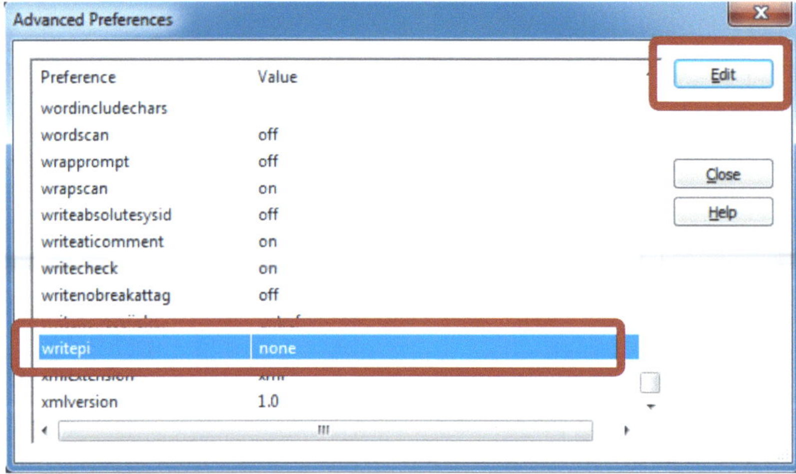

Select **none** from the list and click **OK**.

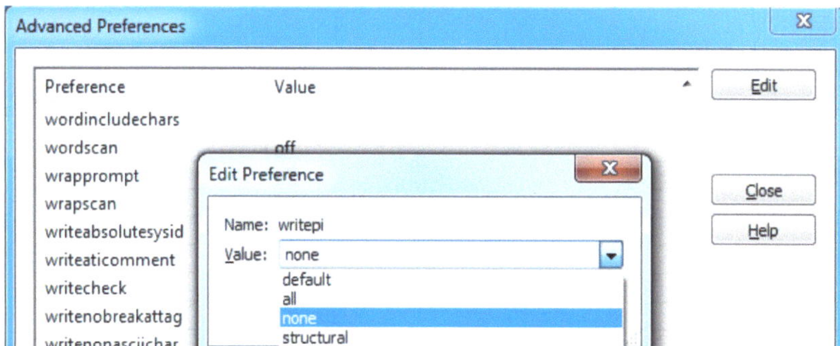

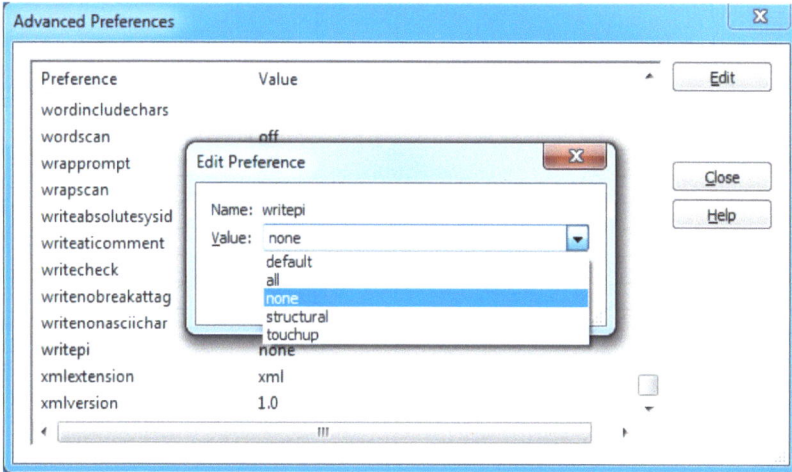

Close the Advanced Preferences window. Click **OK** in the Preferences window.

When you save your file, any processing instructions that were inserted—accidentally or on purpose—will be removed before the file is saved.

Chapter 6. Step 4: Install fonts

Arbortext supports any TrueType and Type 1 PostScript fonts installed on your system. By default, Arbortext will look for fonts on your system. This is true for Arbortext Editor, Styler, and Publishing Engine.

It's a good practice to make sure that any fonts you want to embed in your published PDFs or use in the Editor are installed on your system and on the system that houses the Publishing Engine. As long as the fonts are installed, you can minimize any hassles you might find proofing your published output later on.

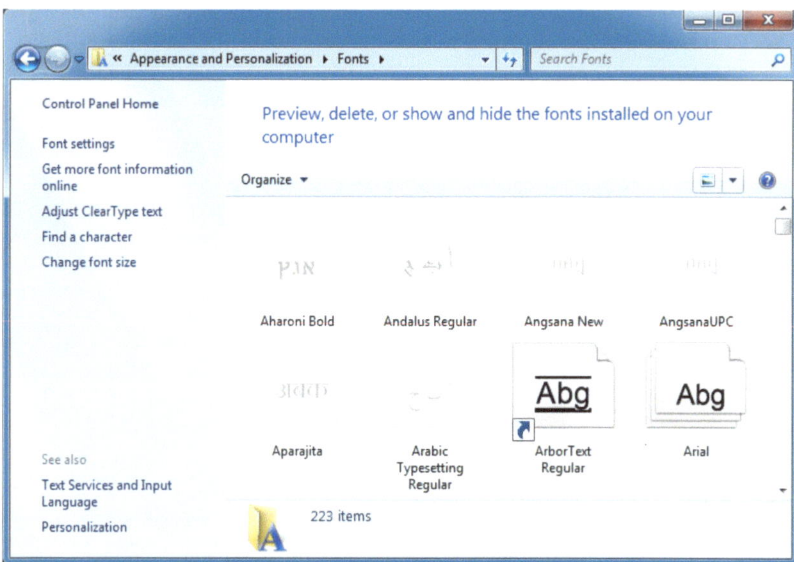

If your fonts aren't behaving correctly, search the help files for "Font configuration."

Chapter 7. Get Started

Topics Covered in this Chapter

♦ Do the tutorials
♦ Take the eLearning courses

You are now ready to go!

At this point, your editing environment is ready for anything you want to do. It's set up for you to configure to fit your preferences and your team's needs. If you want to customize the environment, you're ready for that, too. Everything you need is in place for you to create your own profile variables and create your own stylesheets.

You're also ready for collaboration. You've connected to Windchill and set up everything you need to store your Arbortext technical content into a standard library structure.

Do the tutorials

Arbortext Editor includes a basic tutorial that can get you started quickly. You can find it in the Help Center. The Help Center is the application that contains the complete set of Arbortext help documentation. The Help Center comes standard with Arbortext Editor (starting with 5.4 F000).

You can launch the Help Center directly from Arbortext Editor, or separately by going to the **Start Menu→PTC→Help Center** in Windows.

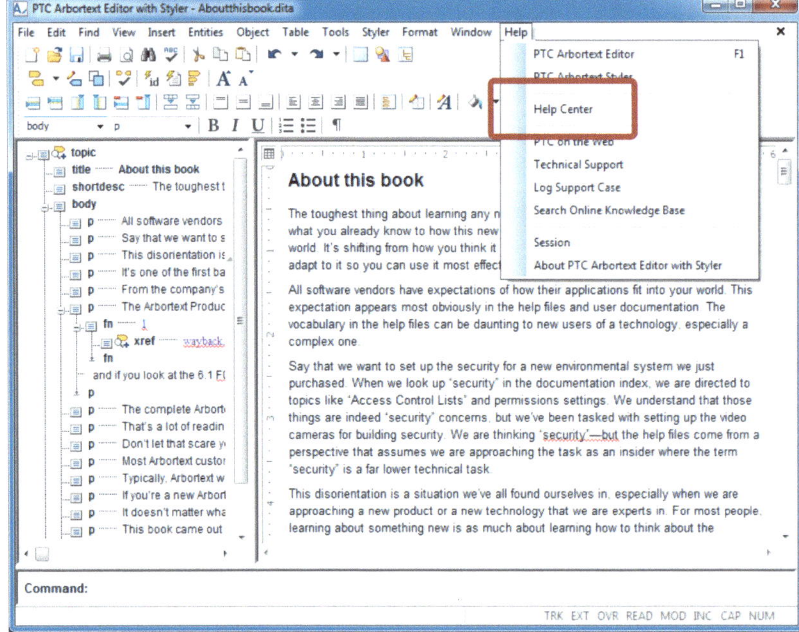

The tutorial can be found under the Authoring section of the Table of Contents:

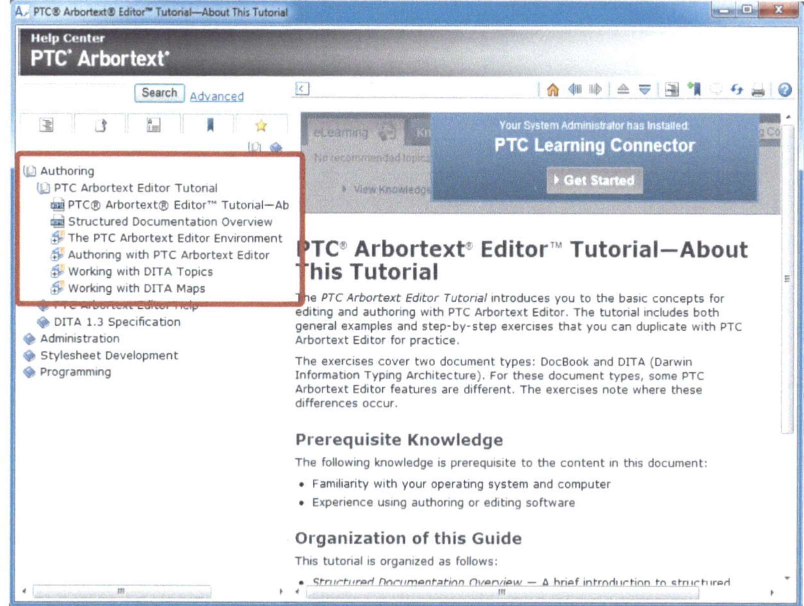

Take the eLearning courses

Whether you are an author who creates and edits information for use and reuse or a systems analyst involved in designing a new multichannel publishing solution for your organization, begin by learning the fundamentals of XML and multichannel publishing. Arbortext eLearning Libraries offer the ideal courses for this purpose.

In the Arbortext world, authors and editors are subject matter experts (SMEs) who create, modify, or edit information. They might be technical writers for whom Arbortext is the primary desktop tool or they might be engineers and researchers who will use Arbortext to enter raw data.

This suite of courses is usually offered as a single week of training and prepares authors and editors to work effectively in

Arbortext Editor. With eLearning, you get the same training material organized and presented as if you were taking in-person classes with a live instructor. Instead of taking five work days away from you in a classroom, the eLearning courses break the course content into 1-hour chunks that you can watch as often as you like.

Here are the recommended training courses for everyone:

- Understanding SGML and XML using Arbortext
- SGML, XML and Arbortext - Understanding the Need for Structured Information
- SGML, XML and Arbortext - Structured Application Concepts
- SGML, XML and Arbortext - Structured Authoring Concepts and Product Overview
- Authoring using Arbortext Editor
- Arbortext Editor - Structured Information and Document Structure
- Arbortext Editor - Arbortext Editor End User Orientation
- Arbortext Editor - Working with Structured Markup
- Arbortext Editor - Creating Tables
- Arbortext Editor - Authoring and Editing Management Tools and Final Workshop
- Introduction to DITA

I always include the Introduction to DITA course even for customers who are not working in DITA right away because that course gives you a DTD/Schema context that can help cement your learning. Even if you're not doing DITA now, learning it early can serve you well down the road. If nothing else, think of taking that course as investing in you: If you're looking for a job later on, you'll be able to say you took a course in DITA and know enough to get started working in it. DITA experience will open doors.

When you're searching for courses in the eLearning libraries at ptc.com, you might notice that some course names are slightly different from the ones listed. That's because every time PTC updates the software they also update the course material and they've changed the name of the course slightly over the years. It's more important that you find the course that is conceptually similar to those listed. That's where the good information can be found.

> **Expert tip!**
>
> For conceptual information, it doesn't matter what version of the class you take. In fact, you might find that the best version of the class in the Arbortext eLearning library is the oldest one (5.4 vs. 6.1).
>
> Remember that PTC has been building the eLearning courses one on top of the other and might assume you already know the older stuff. So don't be afraid to watch the older videos. The user interface won't be the same, but you can figure it out (and the information in the older courses is often better).

Courses for stylesheet programmers

If you think you're going to be maintaining your stylesheet, you will want to take some additional courses. Stylesheet developers are responsible for designing, developing, and maintaining Arbortext stylesheets. Arbortext stylesheets are used to format the screen, as well as to format paper, RTF, HTML Help, and other output formats from Arbortext Editor.

These are the recommended training courses for Advanced Developers and XSL stylesheet developers:

- All of the suggested “courses for everybody”
- Introduction to Arbortext Styler
- Intermediate Arbortext Styler
- Introduction to XSLT and XPath
- Configuration for Publishing
- Multichannel Publishing and Distribution Workshop
- Our webinar on best practices for DITA stylesheets (available on YouTube: ditastyle.tcdojo.org)

Expert tip!

Those who plan to design a stylesheet used *only* for Arbortext Editor window display may want to attend only the "Introduction to Arbortext Styler" class. This introductory class contains enough information for you to change the display in the Arbortext Editor window. It stops before moving on to advanced topics necessary to produce print, web, and other output formats.

Installing Arbortext eLearning class files

Courses in the Arbortext eLearning Library require a set of lab/ exercise files ("class files"). The instructions provided for downloading and configuring these files are not ideal, particularly for newer versions of the Windows operating system, such as Windows Vista and later. Here are some simplified instructions.

Extract the class files

The instructions provided with the course seem to indicate that a copy of WinZip is required to extract the files. This is unnecessary for versions of Windows XP or later. Right-click the file and select **Extract All...** from the pop-up menu. You will be prompted to select a folder into which to extract the files. Either type in the folder name or browse for it using by clicking the button on the right.

To avoid problems, especially with the increased level of security in Windows Vista and later, select a folder in your personal **Documents** folder, which is usually something like:

C:\Users\<your-account-name>\Documents

In Windows XP or earlier:

C:\Documents and Settings\<your-account-name>\My Documents.

Once you have selected a folder, click **Extract**.

Configure Arbortext Editor to find the class files

Some courses include special instructions for extracting files to the root of your **C:** drive (or whatever drive you installed Arbortext Editor to) so that the files will end up in the installation directory for Editor. This is a poor practice. There's a better way to do this.

Extract all of the files to one location. Then, edit your APTCUSTOM environment variable to tell Arbortext Editor where to find the files.

Locate the **custom** directory inside the extracted class files directory. Add the path to this new custom directory at the beginning of your APTCUSTOM variable value and follow it with a semicolon to separate it from what is already there. Then, restart Arbortext Editor (close all windows and re-launch the application).

Whenever you change an environment variable, you must restart Arbortext Editor. You can't change environment variable values while Editor or Styler is running. If you change environment variables while Editor and Styler are running, it will have no effect until you restart the these applications. Close the application, change the variable, and re-launch. You will then have access to all of the files needed to complete the exercises as instructed by the course.

Chapter 8. Top Arbortext resources

Although this is the first book on Arbortext that is not part of the software user documentation, there have always been resources available to members of the Arbortext community.

We are a large community. In 2005, at the last AUGI (Arbortext User Group International) Conference held by Arbortext at Disney World's Contemporary Resort, there were over 800 attendees. As with any conference, attendees make up a small fraction of the user base. Although there aren't the same numbers attending PTC's conference, the user base is still there and still actively sharing information with each other. You can find many of us in forums and various groups online.

No book for the new Arbortext user would be complete without a list of resources available. I know things change, but at this time, all of these resources have been around more than 4 years (one more than 20!), so I feel confident including them here. Even older content often has value. When you've been using something for 20 years, you take a lot of knowledge for granted. Frequently, we tell customers to watch some of the old content in the PTC eLearning library for exactly that reason. Things that were explained when the technology was new aren't explained 20 years later. The user interfaces and features may have changed over time, but the underlying technology and information hasn't.

Everyone learns differently. Some of us are video learners. Some of us prefer books. Some are tactile and need to touch, feel, and move things around. Some of us learn through discussion. As with Arbortext, there's always more than one way to get something done.

Here is the list of resources every Arbortext user should know about:

Additional Arbortext 101 Resources

Location: http://arbortext.training

With the books you have everything you need for success, but sometimes you want a little more. This website has access to the training videos that go along with this book as well as other links. It also provides links to book time with the author: Ask your individual questions in a private, one-on-one consulting session.

Arbortext Forum @ PTC Communities

Location: www.ptcusercommunity.com/community/arbortext

The best thing about this forum is that PTC/Arbortext software engineering staff monitors the forum. Many long-time users and tools folks also regularly monitor the forum. Beginning and advanced questions are encouraged. If you have a question, it's a great resource.

This forum also contains archives from the long-running Arbortext mailing list. Before it got moved to PTC Communities, the PTC/User portal hosted the long-running Adepters mailing list that had been hosted by Arbortext, Inc prior to acquisition by PTC. Originally called "adepters" after "Adept," the original name of Arbortext Editor, this mailing list has been active since 1996, five years after the product was first released in 1991. The entire archive is now contained in the Arbortext Forum at PTC Communities.

Arbortext TC Dojo @ Single-Sourcing Solutions

Location: tcdojo.org

The TC Dojo has a special Arbortext Edition and sponsors an Arbortext Mastermind group. The TC Dojo is a series of webinars in which the topics are chosen by the community and driven by community needs. In the TC Dojo-Arbortext Edition, we cover topics of interest to Arbortext users. Sessions are free.

The Arbortext On-Demand Channel at Vimeo provides recordings of the live Arbortext TC Dojo sessions at low cost to the public. Members of the Arbortext Mastermind group have access for free through the membership forums. The Mastermind Group is members-only. The group meets monthly and is focused on Arbortext user issues. The group is part discussion group, part support group, part networking, and part training. It is governed by the members and has been described as, “more useful than I ever could have imagined.”

At the moment, there are two groups in the TC Dojo that Arbortext users may find of interest: Arbortext Mastermind and Windchill Mastermind. The Windchill group is for IT staff and is more focused on their needs than the end user’s needs. End-user Windchill issues come up in the Arbortext Mastermind group. This group is not free. Members discuss real business issues and confidentiality is required. As a result, there is a small fee to attend to guarantee that random attendees are excluded.

Arbortext Code Archive @ Single-Sourcing Solutions

Location: members.single-sourcing.com : Arbortext User Forum

Over the years, members of the adepters mailing list (see resource #1) have found that they refer to several historical posts on a regular basis. To simplify their own information retrieval and to preserve that knowledge in a neutral location, they created a website pulling the best of the archive out and posting it there. In 2008, the user who created the archive changed careers and passed the site to Single-Sourcing Solutions, the only company to volunteer to migrate the site and sponsor this public benefit. Today, it's in the TC Dojo Forums, but publicly available. If you're creating custom applications on top of your Arbortext environment, the code archive includes some good information.

Arbortext User Groups @ everywhere

The Arbortext User Group has a good presence online. There's a forum @ PTC Communities, a LinkedIn group, a Facebook Group, a Meetup Group, and a YouTube channel with copies of recordings from online meetings.

PTC Communities: ptccommunity.arbortextuser.org

LinkedIn: linkedin.arbortextuser.org

Facebook: facebook.arbortextuser.org

YouTube: youtube.arbortextuser.org

Meetup: meetup.arbortextuser.org

You can find Arbortext users everywhere. Sometimes you just need a little hint on where to start looking.

Expert tip!

Everything Arbortext In One Place @ Arbortext Users blog

Location: everything.arbortextuser.org

Everything you need to know about Arbortext is condensed and explained in this one place. This page was created when the Wikipedia page on Arbortext underwent a hasty deletion. In addition to a lot of historical information, this page documented things the Arbortext user needs to know to successfully navigate the PTC Arbortext channel.

Arbortext Mentoring @ Single-Sourcing Solutions

Our customers want to do it themselves, but they don't want to do it alone. If you're reading this book then you, too, probably want to do it yourself.

As you develop your Arbortext technical and conceptual skills, you might still have questions, or develop new ones. No book or video can cover every situation. You can always email us (info@single-sourcing.com) if you have general questions. Getting answers to questions that are specific-to you often require context and conversation. One way to facilitate that is to sign up for some kind of mentoring.

Think of going from journeyman to apprentice. You're working hard to grow your skills. You can't ask questions of a video or a book and sometimes you can't wait for days to get an answer from public forums. Our customers have found that a mentorship relationship boosts their confidence and helps them climb the learning curves faster.

Each of us at Single-Sourcing Solutions earned our expertise through carefully guided training that we received at the hands of mentors and talented coaches. Today, we are the mentors and coaches to our customers. Our mentoring services support the do-it-yourselfer as much as we support our full-service clientele.

We know that you want to take ownership of your project, your tools, and your content. Ultimately, you need to know how to maintain, grow, and extend them as your environment changes. When you work with a mentor, you don't simply outsource all that learning and responsibility. We help you to take ownership.

Afterword

Thanks for reading. We hope the book has been useful.

If you enjoyed it, you might be ready to advance to **Arbortext 102: Best Practices for Creating Arbortext Styler Stylesheets**. It's all about how to create multi-channel stylesheets for Arbortext publishing.

Join our mailing list and you'll find out when our next book, **Arbortext 103: Best Practices for Configuring, Managing, and Publishing Arbortext Content with the PTC Server**, is ready! We're working on it now, so stay tuned!

Join our mailing list to get tips every month and get notified when our next books are ready: mailinglist.single-sourcing.com

Everyone at Single-Sourcing Solutions participates in community projects—and we have a lot of them! To take advantage of one of our public service projects, go to social.single-sourcing.com and pick the one that works best for you.

You can always reach us directly, too. Email us at info@single-sourcing.com. We're here to help.

Index

C

D

E

F

G

H

I

L

M

P

R

Z

www.ingramcontent.com/pod-product-compliance
Lightning Source LLC
Chambersburg PA
CBHW041314210326
41599CB00008B/270